THE "NEW" TERRORISM

THE "NEW" TERRORISM
MYTHS AND REALITY

Thomas R. Mockaitis

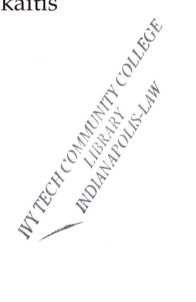

PRAEGER SECURITY INTERNATIONAL
Westport, Connecticut • London

Library of Congress Cataloging-in-Publication Data

Mockaitis, Thomas R., 1955–
    The "new" terrorism: myths and reality / Thomas R. Mockaitis.
p. cm.
    Includes bibliographical references and index.
    ISBN 0–275–98963–1 (alk. paper)
1. Terrorism. 2. Terrorism—History. 3. Terrorism—Prevention. 4. War on Terrorism, 2001–
I. Title.
HV6431.M628 2007
363.325—dc22   2006026014

British Library Cataloguing in Publication Data is available.

Library of Congress Catalog Card Number: 2006026014

ISBN: 0–275–98963–1
ISBN13: 978–0–275–98963–7

First published in 2007

Praeger Security International, 88 Post Road West, Westport, CT 06881
An imprint of Greenwood Publishing Group, Inc.
www.praeger.com

Printed in the United States of America

The paper used in this book complies with the
Permanent Paper Standard issued by the National
Information Standards Organization (Z39.48-1984).

10 9 8 7 6 5 4 3 2 1

To Martha, Nathan, Steven, and Luke

Contents

Preface

Every book is a collaborative effort no matter whose name goes on the cover. Authors build upon and extend the research of other scholars, they work in academic institutions that support their research, and live in families and communities that encourage and care for them as people. To varying degrees all those who enable the writer deserve some credit for his/her publications. The older I get the more my debt of gratitude seems to increase, not necessarily because more people help me but perhaps because I see all those who do more clearly.

I am fortunate to work at DePaul University, which embraces a broad definition of scholarship and believes that teaching extends beyond the walls of a classroom. The University not only funds my research and encourages me to share it with the larger community but in ways small and large enables me to do the variety of tasks that make up my vocation. My students energize my studies and together with my own sons remind me to care about the state of the world beyond my own lifetime. For the past four years I have taught Civil and Military response to terrorism as part of a wonderful team of individuals from the Center for Civil-Military Relations of the Naval Post Graduate School. These individuals and the many military and civilian personnel we have taught around the world have enriched my understanding of terrorism enormously. Chicago's television and radio stations, particularly WGN TV with whom I have worked closely since 9/11, have allowed me to share what I have learned with the wide public audience, for whom I have written this book.

I also belong to a vibrant faith community, Winnetka Presbyterian Church, whose members continually support my vocation. Through many adult education classes and in countless individual conversations their ideas, insights, and questions have helped guide my study of terrorism. Other congregations and civic groups have also invited me to speak and teach classes that have generated more ideas and raised new concerns. The most vibrant discussion of vital issues today may be occurring less in colleges and universities than in churches, mosques, and synagogues.

My family continues to surround me with the love and support without which I could not have completed this or any other project. Having long ago encouraged my study of history, my mother now comes over to cook a meal, check on her grandson, and feed the dog during my trips abroad. Since I published my first book sixteen years ago, my three little boys have grown into fine young men, and my wife and I have celebrated twenty-six wonderful years of marriage. Their presence even more than their many acts of help and kindness makes possible the work that I do.

Introduction

On the morning of September 11, 2001, I was driving my 12-year-old son to school when news that an airliner had struck the south tower of the World Trade Center came over the radio. "It's probably a terrorist attack," Luke concluded. "No," I replied, "It's probably just some poor guy in a Piper Cub learning how to fly." I arrived home just in time to see the second plane strike the north tower. My son had been right. The phone rang almost immediately. WGN TV News asked me to come in to the studio and provide commentary on the unfolding events. I spent the next thirteen hours at the station and have returned countless times in the weeks, months, and years since. Out of that media work grew the idea for this book.

In my many TV appearances, radio interviews, and public lectures, I have consistently encountered a single pressing issue: the need for basic information devoid of hype and untainted by political rhetoric. An educated, non-academic audience wants and needs clear and accurate information on the terrorist threat and how to respond to it. A book that aims to provide such information should neither oversimplify nor needlessly complicate the nature of terrorism in the contemporary world. It should, however, address popular conceptions and misconceptions in a systematic way, replacing rumor and speculation with evidence and analysis. Above all it should seek to dispel the generalized climate of fear stemming largely from ignorance and in some cases deliberately manipulated for political gain. "Fear," an old Dutch saying has it, "is a bad counselor." Unfortunately, that unreliable advisor has had the public ear for far too long.

The title of this book defines its approach. Let me make clear from the outset: I am not declaring terrorism to be a myth; quite the contrary, a real threat certainly exists. Nor do I deny that what the pundits commonly call the *new* terrorism does differ in key respects from what has gone before. Instead I argue that popular perceptions of terrorism contain an undesirable blend of myth and reality. This noxious mix has kept people in a state of needless agitation and unhealthy anxiety. Anxiety in turn hinders serious assessment of real risks and rational consideration of how best to address them. Without such a sober cost-benefit analysis, we are consigned to wasting millions of dollars on measures that make us feel better without offering any real security. The response to the London Underground bombings of July 2005 offers a poignant illustration of this problem. For a month after the attack the city of Chicago put extra police and bomb detection dogs on its elevated platforms to counter the remote possibility of another bomb attack. Because the police could not possibly cover every stop at all times, the extra security would have been easy to evade had an actual operation been planned. Of course, no attack occurred, convincing many observers that the precautions justified the expense. In reality the taxpayers bought an expensive placebo.

The design of the book supports its goal. Each chapter begins by identifying prevailing myths, misconceptions, and oversimplifications about a specific aspect of terrorism. The remainder of the chapter then addresses each issue in detail. Chapters 1–3 progress from a theoretical discussion of the nature of terrorism through a historical overview to an analysis of patterns and trends. Chapters 4–5 focus specifically on al-Qaeda, its origins, organization, evolution, and ideology. Chapters 6–7 assess the terrorist threat and consider how best to respond to it. Chapter 8 examines the U.S. strategy for combating terrorism, considers its effectiveness, and offers an alternative approach.

A few broad themes run through the book as a whole. First, I maintain that much of what passes for "new" terrorism has a long history. Even those aspects of the problem that have not appeared before represent the culmination of trends developing over time. The increasing lethality of terrorism, which so many experts note, is a case in point. Individual terrorist attacks have grown more deadly (although terrorist campaigns have not) but not necessarily for the reasons commonly given: religious fanaticism. Media coverage blended with prime-time TV continually raises the threshold of violence. A dozen deaths no longer shock us the way they once did, so terrorists (like movie producers) up the ante by serving up more mayhem. The globalization of terrorism too represents an evolving trend rather than an entirely new phenomenon. Terrorism has always had an international dimension. In the 1920s the Irish Republican Army depended on support from the Irish American community. During the more recent "Troubles" in Northern Ireland (1969–98) the organization continued to receive support from the expatriate community but also linked up with the Basque separatist organization Basque Fatherland and Liberty (ETA, from the initials of its Basque name, *Euzkadi Ta Askatasuma*) and eventually received help from the Libyan government. In many ways al-Qaeda represents the latest stage in the evolution of terrorism. It has indeed gone global for the same reasons McDonald's, Toyota, and IBM have: air travel, satellite television, and the Internet have knitted the world more tightly together.

This book also challenges most emphatically the idea of a "Global War on Terrorism (GWOT)," which has become one of the most socially enervating and politically debilitating phenomena in recent history. If the word "war" served only as a metaphor for a protracted and difficult struggle, I would have little quarrel with its use. GWOT, however, has become in the eyes of many a real war but a war with no clear definition of an attainable victory. The state of war has been used to justify actions ranging from wiretapping without warrants to drilling for oil in the Alaskan wilderness. Politicians have manipulated the fear it engenders to get elected (or reelected). Besides being socially and emotionally debilitating, fear is expensive. To the billions of dollars spent on military action and necessary security must be added millions more spent on worthless measures that create a temporary sense of well-being without making people safer. The health care costs from stress-related illness and anxiety disorders in the general population may never be measured but are certainly high.

Rejecting GWOT necessitates reexamining the current approach to dealing with the terrorist threat. Rather than conventional war, I argue that counterinsurgency might be a better model for combating terrorism. Such an approach emphasizes addressing the root causes of terrorism while using limited military and extensive police resources in a protracted struggle to wear down al-Qaeda and its affiliates. This strategy also requires us to face an unpleasant but inescapable fact: the scourge of terrorism can no more be eliminated than can crime or poverty. We can and must work to reduce the threat to an acceptable level, but at some point we have to learn to live with it. Terrorism like violent crime has become a permanent part of the social landscape. Far from paralyzing us, this truth may in fact set us free. I can say with virtual certainty that the United States will suffer another terrorist attack, possibly a catastrophic one, in the foreseeable future. I can also add that the chance of any individual American being the victim of such an attack is remote, far less than the chance of dying in an automobile accident, less even than the odds of being struck by lightening. This realization should not make us complacent, but it can enable us to go about our daily lives with less worry.

CHAPTER 1

Madness and Meaning: Understanding the Threat

Prevailing Myths

To most people who saw airliners slam into the World Trade Center and the Pentagon on 9/11 the idea that terrorism is hard to define must seem absurd. And yet, the very emotion that such attacks evoke makes objective understanding difficult. The popular media and even government officials add to the confusion by labeling any form of objectionable political violence "terrorism." However, since formulating a strategy requires an understanding of the enemy, we must begin by examining the nature of terrorism. Such an examination can replace competing and usually impracticable theoretical definitions with a functional one that clearly distinguishes terrorism from other forms of political violence.

Most current definitions classify an act as terrorism based on three broad criteria: target, weapon, and perpetrator. Virtually all experts agree that indiscriminate attacks on civilians constitute terrorism. They also consider use of certain weapons deemed illegitimate by the international community as terrorism. Finally, most experts assess the legitimacy, goals and objectives of the perpetrators in deciding whether or not to declare their actions "terrorism." Unfortunately, each criterion and any combination of the three present serious problems. Terrorists do deliberately attack civilians but so did all belligerents in World War II. Strategic bombing aimed specifically at breaking enemy morale by destroying heavily populated cities and killing their inhabitants. On the other hand, the suicide bombing of the Marine barracks in Lebanon (1983) and the attack on the U.S.S. Cole were widely called terrorism, even though the targets were military. As for means, the West considers certain weapons illegitimate (car bombs, chemical agents, pathogens, etc.). However, the history of warfare provides numerous examples of weapons like the submarine first being considered immoral and later winning general acceptance as legitimate. Many people outside the West consider standoff weapons against which they have no defense illegitimate. Dubbing the suicide bomber "the poor man's cruise missile" makes this point abundantly clear. Finally, definitions based on the legitimacy of the perpetrators and their objectives are bound to be at least somewhat subjective. Spaniards generally applauded ETA's assassination of General Francisco Franco's successor but turned out in droves to protest the Basque organization's bombing of a Barcelona shopping mall in 1987.

Faced with these problems in defining terrorism, most states adopt definitions so broad as to be all-inclusive but terribly unhelpful. The current U.S. military definition of terrorism illustrates this point:

> The calculated use of unlawful violence or the threat of unlawful violence to inculcate fear; intended to coerce or to intimidate governments or societies in the pursuit of goals that are generally political, religious, or ideological.[1]

This definition certainly covers all forms of terrorism. It fails, however, to distinguish terrorism from other forms of political violence. Such an approach makes the term a wax nose, bendable to fit any situation, and perhaps that is what politicians prefer. To further complicate matters, nine departments of the federal government have come up with nine different definitions of terrorism.

The United Nations (UN) has struggled for years to agree on a common definition of terrorism. Two issues consistently block consensus: inclusion of acts of terror by states and the insistence by some members that any definition distinguish between the acts of terrorists and those whom they consider "freedom fighters." Many also express the justifiable concern that efforts to combat terrorism may erode human rights that the organization has consistently fought to uphold. Faced with this seemingly insurmountable impasse, the organization continues to expand the legal framework for combating terrorism. Currently twelve international conventions define and outlaw specific terrorist acts ranging from hijacking to bombings.[2] Useful as this approach may be in combating terrorism, it does not offer much guidance in understanding terrorism or its root causes. The international community has been no more successful than individual states or academic institutions in formulating a common definition of terrorism.

Toward Greater Clarity

Faced with this seemingly endless and largely academic debate, the average person might well paraphrase Supreme Court Justice Potter Stewart's comment about pornography. "I may not be able to define terrorism, but I sure know it when I see it!" This general consensus about what it looks like points the way both to defining terrorism more clearly and to combating it effectively. We need a functional rather than a

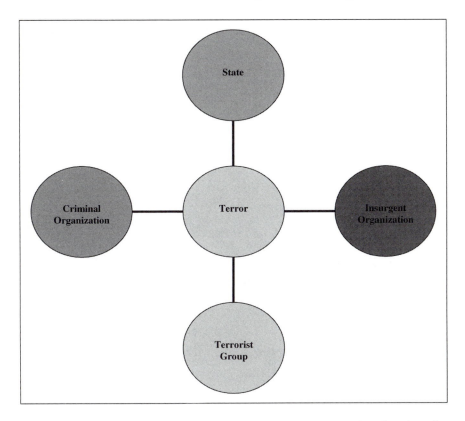

Figure 1.1: Terror is a weapon of choice used by a variety of actors for different purposes.

theoretical definition of the problem. To use a simple analogy, a hunter pursuing a dangerous animal does not need to know its genus, species, and phylum, but he/she must be able to clearly recognize the beast and be intimately acquainted with its behaviors and vulnerabilities. This practical knowledge allows the hunter to predict the quarry's actions and ultimately bag it. The place to begin in fashioning a functional definition is not with *terrorism* but with *terror*, a *weapon* that can be used by a variety of actors.

Making a clear distinction between acts of terror and the organizations that perpetrate them immediately reveals a fundamental problem with a "war on terror." Nations and alliances can attack organizations, but they cannot make war on a weapon such as terror. To mount such attacks, they must understand the nature of the weapon and, more importantly, the nature and characteristics of the organizations that use it. Focusing on actors that use terror to achieve political goals has the added advantage of leading to a functional definition, a pragmatic understanding of the enemy not unlike that used by a hunter. The hunter has little need for an academic definition of the animal he pursues, but he must be able to recognize it, understand its behavior, and know its vulnerabilities.

Terror, unlike most weapons, aims not merely to destroy enemy combatants, but to spread fear among the general population. "Terror," one commentator observed, "is a theater. Its real targets are not the innocent victims but the spectators."[3] Those who watch consist of an audience in the community under attack and an audience in the community from which the terrorists come. To the public in the targeted country terrorists say, "See, no matter how powerful you may be, we can hit you whenever and wherever we choose!" To their own supporters they proclaim, "We are not powerless. We can deal decisive blows against our enemies."

Contrary to one popular myth, terrorist attacks are never completely arbitrary. Those who use terror select targets less for their military value than for their symbolic significance. They choose buildings or landmarks that represent power, pride, or economic strength. They kill people to send a message to the group those people represent. Their means range from conventional explosives to nuclear, biological, or chemical agents. They employ two types of terror. "Enforcement terror" keeps their followers or citizens in line; "agitational terror" attacks their declared enemies.[4] As illustrated in Figure 1.1, terror can be used by a variety of actors: nation states, insurgent movements, criminal organizations, and terrorist groups. An effective operational definition must clearly distinguish between these actors.

State Terror

States employed terror centuries before anyone else. Following the Spartacus slave revolt of the first century BCE, the Romans crucified thousands of captives along the Appian Way, the famous road out of Rome, as a warning to anyone else who considered rebellion. The French Revolution unleashed a "reign of terror" aimed at all enemies of the regime, both real and imagined. The dictators of the twentieth century took state terror to a new level, creating an atmosphere of fear so pervasive as to intimidate any of their subjects out of even contemplating opposition. Soviet Premier Joseph Stalin proved most successful in developing the machinery of state terror also employed by Adolph Hitler, Benito Mussolini, and Francisco Franco. Even contemporary democracies have been accused of "state terrorism." Israel's policies of asymmetrical response to Palestinian attack and collective punishment against entire families for the behavior of individual members are a case in point. The use of aerial bombardment (which always results in some civilian deaths) by the United States against Serbia, Afghanistan, and Iraq has also been criticized.

However reprehensible, terror perpetrated by states against their own people does not destabilize the international system. The difficult task of opposing such abuses belongs in the realm of international human rights advocates. States, alliances, and the United Nations generally focus on terror employed by non-state actors. Even in this arena, however, these actors must be clearly distinguished from one another. The greatest confusion in the current struggle lies in distinguishing between terror employed by insurgents and terror employed by organizations whose goals are so idealistic as to be virtually unattainable. It is for this second group that the term "terrorist" should be reserved. Criminal organizations, a third group, also use terror to keep their own people in line and to intimidate outsiders for various purposes.

Insurgent Terror

Insurgency remains one of the most persistent and intractable forms of conflict. Because of the stigma attached to the term, threatened states often refer to insurgents as terrorists, even though insurgent goals and methods differ markedly from those of terrorist organizations. Calling insurgents "terrorists" for propaganda purposes adds to the confusion surrounding the nature of both forms of conflict.

Insurgency is an organized movement to take over a state from within through a combination of propaganda, guerrilla warfare, and terrorism. Although insurgents have embraced a variety of broad ideologies, they have decidedly focused political goals. Like a virus attacking a cell from within, they seek political power within a nation state by overthrowing an established government. Insurgents feed on grievances within a population, persuading those who feel their government does not meet their basic needs that it must be replaced with one that does. Economic grievances have provided the greatest grist for the insurgents' mill followed closely by ethnic nationalism. Chinese peasants supported (or at least accepted) Mao Tse-Tung not out of love for communism but out of despair over their lives ever getting better. The average Vietnamese saw Americans continuing French Colonial rule. He fought a war of independence, not a crusade for communism. Sometimes economic and ethnic nationalist motives complement one another. The Provisional Irish Republican Army fought for unification of Northern Ireland with the Republic of Ireland. The appalling conditions, limited opportunities, and rampant discrimination under which most Catholics lived encouraged them to support the insurgents.

Whatever the grievances that promote unrest, insurgents mobilize support for their cause through propaganda or, to use a more neutral term, "information warfare." They dispense information through various means, pointing out the shortcomings of the existing government and explaining how things will be better once the insurgents gain power. They also publicize every atrocity or excess government forces commit in combating the insurgency. Without such political mobilization, insurgency cannot exist. Economic hardship may lead to violence on a massive scale, as in the case of medieval peasant revolts, but without "a common vocabulary of hope and protest," no insurgent movement can succeed.[5]

Insurgents make use of terror, but they do so selectively. Since their success depends in large measure on winning the support or at least the acceptance of the general population, they seek to avoid actions that alienate people. They target government facilities, assassinate officials, and murder ordinary people who aide the authorities, but they generally avoid inflicting mass casualties. Insurgent terror must send a clear message that certain acts will be punished and that the threatened government can do nothing to protect people from such retribution. It must not, however, be so indiscriminate or pervasive as to alienate people from the insurgency. Insurgent terror can also provoke the government into using force so indiscriminately as to further alienate disaffected people and drive them into the arms of the insurgents. Iraqi insurgents, for example, have become quite skilled at firing at American patrols from within the homes of noncombatants, knowing full well that such tactics will bring a barrage of return fire that kills innocent civilians.[6] Provoking a heavy handed response may also win the insurgents international support, which can lead to recognition and even intervention on their behalf. This strategy worked brilliantly in Kosovo during the late 1990s. The Kosovo Liberation Army provoked the regime of Slobodan Milošević into conducting yet another round of ethnic cleansing, which brought the wrath of the North Atlantic Treaty Organization (NATO) down on Serbia and landed Milošević in The Hague.

A clear distinction between terror and guerrilla warfare, both of which insurgents employ, must be made. Guerrilla (Spanish for "small war") warfare involves irregular forces operating (alone or in support of conventional armies) out of uniform and in loose formations. Historically guerrillas have attacked small regular military units, isolated outposts, police, and government paramilitary forces. Guerrillas used hit-and-run tactics, striking when opportunity arose and then melting back into the general population. Unlike guerrilla operations, terrorist attacks target the general population. The Pentagon's decision to broaden the definition of terrorism to include attacks on U.S. military barracks in the Khobar Towers (Riyadh, Saudi Arabia) and the U.S.S. Cole in Aden harbor has contributed to the already considerable confusion between terrorism and guerrilla warfare.

Criminal Terror

Criminal organizations like insurgents will make limited use of terror to achieve their objective. Since that objective consists almost entirely of making money, however, they use force even more selectively than insurgents. Crime syndicates recognized long ago a threshold of public tolerance below which they must operate to stay in business. As long as their use of terror confines itself to occasional murder of rival members or traitors within their own organizations, no matter how gruesome, such violence will not produce a strong public reaction. However, as the infamous Saint Valentine's Day Massacre in Chicago illustrates, gangland violence can produce sufficient public outrage to produce a government crackdown. Criminal organizations will keep their use of enforcement terror at relatively low levels to avoid unwanted attention.

An exception to this rule may occur when legitimate authority becomes so weak that criminal organizations can gain control of whole sectors of an economy or even territory. The Russian mob took advantage of the collapse of communism to establish itself in the new Russia, providing in some cases the only stability in a chaotic economy. During the early 1990s the mob used violence to a degree rivaling the gang wars of Chicago in the 1920s until it settled into a more "respectable" business mode and exercised the same restraint as its American counterparts. Drug cartels in Colombia have become powerful enough to control entire provinces. They do not hesitate to murder judges and other government officials and even to engage the Colombian Army. Heroin traffickers exercise similar control over the Golden Triangle region of Southeast Asia, and Afghan warlords now control that country's opium production.

These exceptions do not, however, change the general pattern of restraint exercised by criminals. Even in the few extreme cases just noted the criminal gangs and syndicates play by rules. Completely indiscriminate use of terror renders it ineffective as a weapon. People must know which actions will make them a target. For criminals the profit motive reigns supreme, so anyone who interferes with it risks serious harm that will be inflicted in a manner that sends a message to everyone else. In their day-to-day lives organized criminals will often be model citizens, contributing to the welfare of their communities and even dispensing rough justice to protect those communities.

Terrorist Groups

If terror is indeed a weapon, can there truly be such a thing as terror*ism*? The suffix "ism" denotes an ideology or ideological movement. By that standard "terrorism" should be the elevation of terror to a system of thought, indiscriminate violence for its own sake with no larger political or other purpose. Such a definition makes no sense even for the most lunatic fringe organizations. However, we still need to distinguish between insurgent and criminal groups who make limited use of terror to achieve focused objectives (political or pecuniary) and extremist organizations who use terror in less discriminating ways for more diffuse or abstract goals.

In the aftermath of 9/11 analysts have bandied about a number of terms to describe what they see as the "new terrorism." Adjectives like "religious," "millenarian," "apocalyptic," and "fantasy-ideology" have been placed before "terror" or "terrorism." A perceived irrationality links each of these definitions. The *new* terrorism, so the logic goes, pursues broad, ideological/religious goals so utopian as to be unattainable in the real world. With God on their side or at least with an unshakable faith in some vision of the future behind them, these zealots kill in pursuit of their millenarian vision, restrained only by the means at their disposal. Al-Qaeda asserts that the civilians in the Twin Towers deserved to die because they were the architects of western imperial capitalism at war with Islam worldwide. Television footage of people jumping to certain death rather than be burned alive certainly reinforced the popular belief that such terrorists have little regard for life.

Distinguishing terrorism (or terrorist organizations) from insurgency (or insurgent organizations) based entirely or even primarily upon religious motivation poses serious problems. First of all, anyone who considers religiously motivated terror to be new should consider the origin of the word "zealot," a term applied to a group of Jewish rebels against Roman rule who used tactics, such as poisoning wells, which today would be considered terrorism.[7] Historically, however, religion has usually been part of the terrorists' "ethno/nationalist" identity, not the primary force motivating their activities.[8] Furthermore, most religious extremists do not use terror as extensively or indiscriminately as does al-Qaeda. The Christian Identity Movement in the United States includes some groups and individuals who perpetrated terrorist attacks and many others who have expressed a willingness to do so. Their terror, however, has been limited and focused. Even Timothy McVeigh and Terry Nichols targeted the Murrah Federal Building in Oklahoma City not to produce mass casualties (although they were willing to accept such loss of life) but to destroy a symbol of what they saw as an oppressive government and those who worked for it. Nonetheless, while the two should not be equated, religious extremism does fuel much contemporary terrorism.[9]

Religious motivation alone does not then separate terrorism from insurgency. Again, the hunting metaphor commends itself as the best means of distinguishing between them: how does a terrorist organization look and behave differently from an insurgent one? The key distinction may be the degree to which that organization relies on terror as its weapon of choice rather than in how deadly its attacks may be or why it carries them out. An organization that uses terror selectively in support of a larger political strategy that includes a range of tactics (subversion, guerrilla warfare, etc.) to gain control of a government, region, or country deserves to be called "insurgent." An organization that lacks the capacity to do anything but carry out terrorist attacks deserves to be labeled "terrorist."[10] While religious zeal has led groups and individuals to mount horrendous terrorist attacks, other motivations can produce the same result. The Red Army Faction in Germany and the Red Brigades in Italy carried out acts of terror during the 1970s with no possibility of achieving any even remotely concrete objective. An atheist Marxist ideology motivated these two groups, not religion. Nonetheless, terrorist groups who believe that God endorses both their cause and their methods seem far less likely to worry about the consequences of their actions and far more willing to engage in mass killing than ones focused on winning support and seizing political power.

Willingness to negotiate also distinguishes terrorists from insurgents, states, and even criminals. No matter how odious their behavior and regardless of the justness or unjustness of their cause, insurgent organizations and crime syndicates have pragmatic goals. This pragmatism makes them rational actors. Faced with the prospect of defeat or endless struggle on the one hand and a limited victory on the other, such actors usually choose the latter. The Provisional Irish Republican Army (PIRA) offers an excellent example of such pragmatism. Committed to forcing British withdrawal from Northern Ireland as a necessary precondition for unification with the Republic of Ireland, PIRA faced an unpleasant dilemma by the late 1980s. Although the insurgents could carry out their campaign of violence indefinitely, they could never hope to force the British to quit the province. The security forces had achieved what Home Secretary Reginald Maudling had long before dubbed "an acceptable level of violence."[11] PIRA could persist but not progress toward its ultimate goal.[12] The British government had demonstrated an unshakable resolve to remain in Northern Ireland for as long as the majority of men and women in the province wanted them there. The British Army had extensive counterinsurgency experience, which not only prevented PIRA from doing it much damage, but also allowed it to score some stunning successes against the insurgents.

Faced with the prospect of indefinite stalemate and dwindling support for a campaign of violence that seemed to be going nowhere, the insurgents did an about-face. They embraced electoral politics, entered into secret negotiations with the British government, and agreed to a ceasefire in 1994. With fits and starts the truce has held every since, and in 1998 Sinn Fein, the political party associated with PIRA, accepted the Good Friday Accords, a complex proposal for power sharing in Northern

Ireland with a role for both the British and Irish governments to play in the affairs of the province. The 9/11 attacks so discredited the use of terror that a return to violence seems unlikely. The London bombings of July 7, 2005 further undermined the legitimacy of using terror. Within a month of the attacks Sinn Fein leader (and former PIRA member) Jerry Adams announced the decommissioning of weapons.[13] While the Nationalists still embrace the goal of a united Ireland, they accept a share in power and a better life for members of their community as enough "victory" for now.

Terrorist organizations by comparison seem incapable of compromise. They often espouse goals so vague and/or outrageous that no one could ever meet them. Even if a threatened government or the international community were inclined to negotiate with these groups, the terrorists' own ideology often precludes compromise. Religiously motivated terrorists follow a divinely inspired mission that allows for no alteration. To deviate from the chosen course would be sacrilege. The Christian Identity Movement provides a useful example of this attitude. United by a common set of beliefs rather than an overarching organization, its followers desire a return to the early American republic in which Aryan people rule a Christian nation. Beyond this mythical vision of the past, hatred of virtually all other ethnic and religious groups, and opposition to government authority, the movement lacks any coherent strategy with specific goals. Outsiders would be hard pressed to identify any concession(s) that would satisfy such a movement.

Organization

Illicit groups organize themselves to maximize their ability to operate and minimize chance of their detection. Most use some variety of the cell system devised by the Bolshevik revolutionaries in Russia. Clandestine cells of perhaps four members link to the larger organization through only one member, who knows only one person at the next level. Apprehending a cell member directly imperils at most four other people: his or her cell mates and the outside contact, who will break the link as soon as the cell has been compromised. The cell leader may never even meet his contact, communicating with that person through various indirect means. Cells may be somewhat larger and can also be specialized for a variety of functions.[14]

Cells can be arranged in hierarchical or flat organizations. Insurgents enjoying safe havens adjacent to the territory they contest have often based their governing body in that sanctuary. The "general staff" of the Provisional Irish Republican Army directed the insurgency in Northern Ireland from the safety of the Republic of Ireland. The Basque separatists had a sanctuary in France until the 1990s, and communist insurgents in Oman (1970–75) operated out of South Yemen. During the late 1990s al-Qaeda maintained its headquarters and training bases in Afghanistan. Following the U.S. invasion in late 2001, the organization flattened out. Cells loosely networked around the world operate semi-autonomously with perhaps minimal direction from Osama bin Laden and his associates and a general mandate to attack suitable targets. They may even form for a single operation and dissolve in the act of carrying it out as occurred during the London (2005) bombings.

Financing

Any organization, clandestine or otherwise, needs money to operate. States can, of course, fund their activities through legally collected tax revenues. Clandestine operations must use subterfuges or illicit activities to raise money. The funds different types of groups need vary considerably. Insurgents bent upon seizing control of a state may require considerable sums to arm, train, and supply a large guerrilla force ultimately capable of transforming itself into a regular army.[15] Terrorist organizations, however, can achieve a great deal with relatively modest sums.

No matter the amount, raising money for a clandestine group has always presented challenges. Organized crime syndicates deduct expenses from the income generated by their illegal activities, just as any legitimate business would do. Insurgents often received funding from states, especially during the Cold War.[16] The United States and the Union of Soviet Socialist Republics used insurgents and the states they threatened as pawns in a proxy war against one another. The last such conflict took place in Afghanistan (1979–88), where the United States backed Afghan fighters supported by foreign *mujahedeen* against Soviet invaders. Insurgents also receive voluntary contributions from the local population within which they operate and from diaspora communities. The PIRA got weapons and funding from Libya and contributions from the Irish-American community. Cuba and Nicaragua funded the insurgents in El Salvador during the 1980s. Insurgents who control territory can also collect "revolutionary taxes" from the local population.

Insurgents and terrorist organizations also engage in illegal activities to finance their operations. The Revolutionary Armed Forces of Colombia (FARC, from the initials of its Spanish name, *Fuerzas Armadas Revolucionarias de Colombia*) has become a major player in international cocaine trade. Al-Qaeda raised money by selling Afghan opium, and the Madrid bombers used drug money raised by their leader who had converted to radical Islam while in prison on a narcotics charge.[17] Terrorist organizations will also engage in extortion, credit card fraud, and armed robbery to raise money. Seemingly legitimate charities attract the dollars of well-meaning people who often have no idea that their money funds terrorism.

States and Illicit Organizations

Financing raises the larger question of the relationship between states and illicit organizations that make use of terror. Targeting states that "sponsor terrorism" became a priority of the Bush administration after 9/11 without much public discussion of what such sponsorship actually means. While no state sanctions or supports criminal activity, virtually every nation faces the challenge of organized crime. In dealing with this threat to law and order governments engage in cost-benefit analyses. They weigh the damage done by the criminal activity/organization against the cost of eliminating it. Successful criminal organizations have learned to operate just below the threshold of public tolerance. While most publics accept the inevitability of some criminality, they become most concerned about violence. In the 1920s few Americans got worked up over enforcing unpopular prohibition laws against bootleggers, but they found the St. Valentine's Day massacre unacceptable. Al Capone's Chicago mob crossed the line and provoked the Federal government into devoting more resources to fighting the gangsters. Better law enforcement did not eliminate organized crime, but it did push its activities back below the public threshold of tolerance.

Organized crime has become more problematic in the post-Cold War world. The breakup of states in Eastern Europe has produced quasi-independent provinces and new countries small enough to allow criminal organizations to exercise considerable influence if not outright control of territories. The weak, fragmented state of Bosnia has great difficulty resisting organized crime groups that set up shop on its territory. The Kosovo Liberation Army combined insurgency with organized crime, and although it has become a legitimate political party, its involvement in criminal activity persists.

While many states have supported both insurgent groups and terrorist organizations, few have actually sponsored them. *Sponsorship* implies that the state creates, funds, and directs the illicit organization or intentionally provides it a haven. Libya probably sponsored the terrorists who bombed a Berlin discotheque in 1983 and blew up Pan Am Flight 103 in 1988. By allowing al-Qaeda to operate openly on its soil, the Taliban regime in Afghanistan sponsored that organization, although it did not create and may not have controlled it. *Support*, on the other hand, covers a whole range of material and other assistance. Iran supports Lebanese Hezbollah, by supplying money to the organization but does not control its actions. During the 1980s, Libya also supported PIRA, supplying money, explosives, and training bases. The United States supported the Nicaraguan Contras with weapons, money, and probably covert military advising, although it characterized the group as "freedom fighters."

Today the connection between terrorist organizations and states has become more complicated. While few states provide direct assistance to illicit organizations, many cannot prevent such aid being rendered by private individuals, charities, and even sympathetic members of their own governments. Strong indirect evidence suggests that the Royal Ulster Constabulary, frustrated by legal restrictions on fighting PIRA, leaked the names of suspected PIRA members to Protestant paramilitaries, who then murdered the suspects. Saudi Arabia is one of America's closest allies and at the same time a major supporter of terrorism. Although the monarchy supports the U.S. antiterrorism effort, wealthy Saudis have contributed to terrorist organizations. Millions of people around the world contribute to charities that funnel money to illegal organizations with or without the donors' knowledge.

Some states unwittingly provide terrorists safe havens, not because they wish to do so, but because they lack the resources to evict them. The post-Cold War world has given birth to new states and weakened

Table 1.1: Characteristics of states and illicit organizations that use terror.

Actor → Characteristic ↓	State	Insurgent	Criminal	Terrorist
Objective	Political power	Political power	Profit	Utopian goals
Focus	National	National or regional	Transnational or international	Transnational or international
Popular support	Require some support but wider acceptance	Require considerable popular support	Require acceptance	Require some popular support
Organization	Formal and hierarchical	Cells linked hierarchically	Extended family	Flat network of cells and groups
Financing	Tax revenues	Foreign aide, voluntary contributions, Illicit activity	Illicit activity	Foreign aide, voluntary contributions, illicit activity
Degree of terror used	Limited	Limited	Limited	Extensive
Willingness to negotiate	Moderate to high	Moderate to high	Moderate	Low

old ones. Many of these states exercise only limited sovereignty over their own national territory. A weak government in Beirut cannot prevent Hezbollah from attacking Israel from within Lebanese territory. Argentina, Paraguay, and Brazil collectively have been unable to expel terrorist groups from the tri-border region that they share. A standing joke containing more truth than humor has it that although Hamid Karzai has been elected president of Afghanistan, he is really only the mayor of Kabul and even then, only until dark. Even states that exercise real sovereignty over the whole of their national territory inadvertently host sleeper cells or active terrorist groups. Even more countries have the potential for such parasites to infest them as a virus infects a defenseless host.

As Table 1.1 illustrates, actors that employ terror can be broadly distinguished from one another according to seven characteristics: objective, focus, popular support, organization, financing, degree of terror used, and willingness to negotiate.

From Theory to Reality

Few things in the real world fit neatly into categories specified in theoretical models. Although a meaningful distinction between terrorism and insurgency must be drawn, the distinction cannot be made hard and fast. Some organizations exhibit mixed characteristics, and groups change over time. The hunter must understand the beast while recognizing that it is always part chameleon. However, even the evolution of illicit groups sometimes follows predictable patterns.

Insurgency always has a shelf life. Any insurgent organization worthy of the name (i.e., one that enjoys support among disaffected people with legitimate grievances) cannot remain static. If the insurgency grows and the insurgents pursue a coherent strategy, the movement may succeed, occasionally by seizing power but more often by extracting concessions from the government. If support for the insurgency does not grow but the insurgents persist in their campaign of violence, then they have become mere terrorists. The Basque separatist group ETA fits this category. The post-Franco Spanish government granted the Basques every reasonable concession regarding language, culture, and local autonomy. Complete independence Madrid could not grant because half the Basque territory lies in France. By the late 1980s ETA had become an organization capable of little more than senseless acts of violence against innocent civilians.

Insurgencies may also degenerate into mere criminality. Since virtually all insurgent organizations resort to criminal activity to support their activities, this transition can occur quite easily. Extortion, racketeering, robbery, and narcotics trafficking have long funded revolutionary activity.

Insurgents who see their cause failing and even those who have achieved some success can find illegal activity too profitable to forego. This attraction helps explain why splinter groups prefer to continue the struggle long after their comrades put the gun on the shelf. In some cases, however, entire organizations transform themselves into criminal enterprises. The FARC in Colombia now controls a major cocaine producing region and behaves in a manner that makes it almost indistinguishable from the country's other drug cartels. When being in opposition pays so well, why accept the responsibilities of government that inevitably follow an insurgent victory?

The Moral Dimension

Popular and even academic discussion of contemporary political violence often degenerates into meaningless relativism and national self-deprecation on the one hand and demonizing of the enemy on the other. "One man's terrorist is another's freedom fighter," a common cliché has it. "Perhaps we deserved the 9/11 attacks because of our behavior toward the rest of the world," goes another. "*Those* people [the terrorist] are just like that. You can't reason with them," asserts a third. No discussion of insurgency, organized crime, and terrorism would be complete without consideration of the ethical dimension of political violence.

The relativist argument raises the important point that political struggles, violent or otherwise, hinge on legitimacy. The winners often receive a kind of absolution for the acts they committed in gaining power. During the struggle supporters and opponents of a revolutionary movement approve or condemn its action based on whether or not they consider the movement's goals legitimate. The deaths of innocent people caught in the crossfire will be dismissed as tragic but necessary "collateral damage," presuming that the belligerents even accept that there can be such a creature as "an innocent civilian." Perpetrators will also deflect blame for specific incidents by pointing to the larger culpability of the other side. The response of a high ranking PIRA member following the unintended killing of two Catholics in an attack aimed at the security forces illustrates this point:

> The tragedy of this war is that IRA Volunteers, British forces and, sadly, also civilians will continue to suffer and die as long as Britain refuses to accept its fundamental responsibility for what is happening in our country.[18]

Threatened governments will also employ this "look-what-you-made-me-do" logic, as the famous "we had so destroy the village to save it" justification makes clear.

The "one man's freedom fighter is another man's terrorist argument" serves merely to "undercut the natural human antipathy for terrorist methods, and permit terrorist propaganda far more credence than it deserves."[19] Critics of this strong statement will argue that it dismisses the legitimacy of some insurgent goals. This concern may be addressed by separating ends and means. Certain heinous acts can be condemned no matter what cause they serve. International conventions against the use of torture make no exception based on the intentions of the perpetrators. Suicide bombing deserves the same condemnation. Many Palestinians who agree with the goals of Hammas also condemn its terrorist methods.

If justifications for terrorism are naïve, claims that the victims of terror somehow deserved their fate are downright offensive. The best example of such warped reasoning appeared in a 2005 editorial by University of Colorado-Boulder Ethnic Studies Professor Ward Churchill. "On the morning of September 11, 2001," Churchill wrote, "a few more chickens —along with some half-million dead Iraqi children—came home to roost in a very big way at the twin towers of New York's World Trade Center."[20] Churchill went on to assert that, far from being innocent civilians, those who died in the Towers "formed a technocratic corps at the very heart of America's global financial empire." He referred to these men and women as "little Eichmanns."[21] Few academics would stoop to such a base comparison, but the idea that the United States now reaps what it sows can be heard in many universities. Questionable foreign policies have certainly contributed to the environment in which terrorism thrives, but a clear causal relationship between any specific action and the 9/11 attacks would be hard to find. Furthermore, no one in Washington from either party controls the spread of Western secularism with all of its problems and possibilities via the Internet and satellite television. Finally, the idea that civilians deserved to die in the Towers, the Pentagon, or anywhere else, on or after 9/11, is obscene.

The tendency of some elements of the media and even some politicians to blame al-Qaeda terrorism on Islam and/or to view all Muslims as inherently suspect is equally objectionable. The tendency to view Islam as an atavistic religion inherently prone to violence and irrational behavior was common enough prior to 9/11 and has become more widespread since. Such simplistic views actually abet the terrorists who wish to convince Muslims that the "Global War on Terrorism" is really a Western war on Islam.

Conclusion

Terror, a versatile weapon designed to spread fear among those witness it, can be employed by many actors. States have practiced it the longest to discipline their own members. Criminal groups use it to eliminate rivals, keep their own members in line, and intimidate witnesses from testifying against them. Insurgents employ terror selectively as part of a comprehensive strategy to gain control of a country. In contrast, terrorists kill in the service of utopian religious or other ideological goals rather than to achieve a political object. Illicit groups that use terror can be distinguished from one another based on their objectives, organization, and willingness to negotiate for limited gain rather than total victory. Although distinctions between illicit groups that use terror can and must be made, these distinctions are not always hard and fast.

CHAPTER **2**

Terrorism Past and Present

Prevailing Myths

Much discussion of contemporary terrorism suffers from a lack of historical perspective. This a-historical approach encourages two mistaken
notions. First, some observers maintain that terrorism today differs only
by degree from terrorism over past decades or even centuries. Second,
many more people believe that al-Qaeda and its affiliates represent an
entirely new phenomenon. Like most over-generalizations, each assertion
contains some truth and a great deal of error. Contemporary terrorist
organizations developed from past ones, copying their successes, learning
from their mistakes, and adapting their methods and approaches to
changing circumstances. These groups also make use of resources
unavailable to their predecessors. Despite these continuities, however,
contemporary terrorism does have features not present in previous movements, but even this "new" dimension has historical roots.

Understanding terrorism today requires setting it within historical context. A brief chronological survey reveals both continuity and change over
time. Rather than review every terrorist organization in encyclopedic
fashion, this survey needs only to cover representative groups. A historical overview also reveals trends and patterns in the development of terrorism in general and the evolution of contemporary movements and
groups in particular.

Historical Origins

Long before the creation of modern insurgent and terrorist groups,
kingdoms, empires, and states used terror to intimidate their enemies
and keep their subjects in line. The Romans ruled the Mediterranean
world through a skillful combination of generosity and fear. They
rewarded those who supported them and brutally punished those who
rebelled. Entire towns would be sacked, their leaders slaughtered and
ordinary people sold into slavery. Crucifixion was a powerful instrument
of state terror employed to deter crime and discourage rebellion.

Throughout the medieval and early modern periods, public executions served a similar purpose. Anyone watching a man being hanged, drawn and quartered would think twice before committing treason. The "reign of terror" during the French Revolution sent more than 20,000 "enemies of the state" to the guillotine in a matter of months. Criminals who had ears or even hands cut off reminded people of the penalty for stealing. In managing their global empires in the eighteenth and nineteenth centuries, the European powers exercised brutality worthy of the Romans. Following the Sepoy Mutiny in India in the 1850s, British troops lashed captured rebels to boards, strapped them to the muzzles of artillery pieces, and blew them apart in front of an assemblage of Indian troops. They, like most other colonialists, collectively punished entire communities for the behavior of individuals.

Even in conventional conflicts states resorted to terror. During World War II the Germans practiced a policy of *schrecklicheit* (terror) in occupied territories. For every German soldier killed by partisans, the Nazis executed one hundred hostages. The most infamous use of retaliatory terror took place in Czechoslovakia following the assassination of SS Lieutenant General Reinhardt Heidrich by partisans in 1942. In retaliation the SS destroyed the village of Lidice, killing men and boys over fifteen, deporting women and children to concentration camps, and leveling every building.

In the near total wars of the twentieth century, the belligerents attacked civilians to spread terror and break resistance. The Germans equipped the JU87 Stuka dive bomber with sirens to frighten those being bombed. Both Allied and Axis bombing campaigns deliberately targeted civilians in hopes of getting them to pressure their governments to sue for peace. Although aerial bombardment has since become a legitimate weapon of war, the recipients of errant bombs or missiles have every reason to consider themselves victims of terror. They have no ability to defend against or even hide from such standoff weapons.

Finally, modern authoritarian regimes have persistently used enforcement terror to keep their own people in line. The fascist dictators Benito Mussolini and Francisco Franco used terror as an instrument of social control. As soon as he came to power, Adolph Hitler began constructing a formidable machinery of state terror aimed not only at Jews, but at communists, criminals, the asocial, and anyone else deemed an enemy of the German people.[1] State terrorism reached its apogee under Soviet dictator Joseph Stalin. After eliminating his enemies within the Communist Party and purging the Red Army of suspect officers, he turned the extensive system of state terror against the Soviet people. The secret police received quotas of "counter-revolutionaries" to apprehend and send to the forced labor camps of the infamous Gulag system, where many perished. Stalin's minions conducted show trials of prominent suspects and summarily executed countless others.

Long after the fall of these infamous dictators, authoritarian regimes continued to use terror against their own people. In the 1970s a military junta in Argentina conducted a dirty war against left wing dissidents, dumping many far out in the Atlantic Ocean where they swell the ranks of the "disappeared." During the 1980s the government of El Salvador used right-wing paramilitary death squads made up of off-duty army officers to murder political opponents, socially active priests, and anyone else who threatened the rule of the country's oligarchs. Saddam Hussein also made extensive use of state terror to control the Iraqi people. These cases represent but a few examples of what remains a persistent political phenomenon throughout the world.

Non-State Terror in the Modern Era

Use of terror by non-state actors has ancient roots as well. In their first century CE revolt against Roman rule, the Zealots poisoned wells and assassinated their enemies. In India from the eighth to the nineteenth century, religious fanatics known as "Thugs" ambushed and ritually murdered innocent travelers as sacrifices to the goddess Kali. From 1090-1272 the "Assassins" or "hashish eaters" murdered crusaders in the Holy Land. Like some contemporary groups, the Assassins combined drug use with murder. The names of all three groups have become permanent terms naming the type of violent activity in which they specialized.[2]

While these isolated groups illustrate persistent recurrence of terrorism over the centuries, they have no direct connection to the modern use of terror. The systematic use of terror in support of political or ideological movements dates to the second half of the nineteenth century. Both Marxist and ethnic nationalist revolutionary movements used terror to further their goals. Because these revolutionaries targeted rulers and elected leaders they described themselves as "anarchists." Contrary to the general meaning of the term, revolutionary anarchists did not promote chaos for its own sake. Rather they believed that by assassinating heads of state they would further socialist revolution. For these revolutionaries, terror was "propaganda by the deed," a doctrine named for Peter Kropotkin's famous statement, "A single deed is better propaganda than a thousand pamphlets." Another anarchist, Johann Most, observed: "Everyone now knows, from experience, that the more highly placed the one shot or blown up, and the more perfectly executed the attempt, the greater the propagandistic effect."[3]

Another revolutionary writer of this period articulated what would become the perennial argument of extremists: the revolutionary acknowledges no morality but his own. "For him only that is moral which contributes to the triumph of the revolution," wrote Sergei Nechaev in 1868. "All that obstructs this is immoral and criminal."[4] Such logic cannot be countered by rational argument from without. The terrorist, like the religious fanatic, possesses an unshakable faith in his cause and sees disagreement as evidence that the one voicing it has lost faith and must be destroyed.

Anarchists achieved some dramatic successes in the late nineteenth and early twentieth centuries. They assassinated Tsar Alexander II of Russia in 1881, Empress Elizabeth of Austria-Hungary in 1898, and President William McKinley of the United States in 1901. On May 4, 1886, anarchists in Chicago threw a bomb at a line of policeman during a labor rally in Haymarket Square killing several people. Nationalists revolutionaries also murdered political leaders. On June 28, 1914, Gavrilo Princep assassinated Archduke Franz Ferdinand, heir-apparent of the Austro-Hungarian Empire, in Sarajevo, Bosnia. Princep belonged to the Black Hand, a secret organization of Serbian nationalists committed to annexing Bosnia-Herzegovina to the Kingdom of Serbia.

Although assassinations made a dramatic impression, they did nothing to promote the revolutionary cause. In fact, the murders usually proved counterproductive because of the inevitable repression that such acts provoked. Assassination of the Austrian archduke did lead to the outbreak of the First World War but only because of a complex set of circumstances that the assassins did not understand. Princep certainly could not have anticipated and would not have intended that his action would spark a wider European war in which his beloved Serbia would suffer the highest percentage of casualties of any belligerent and be occupied. Neither the assassination of the Tsar nor the murder of the American President accomplished anything.

The ineffectiveness of such isolated acts of terror led Vladimir Lenin, the father of Russian communism, to reject them. In his political treatise "Where to begin?" Lenin stated his position on the use of terror. "In principle we have never rejected, and cannot reject, terror," he asserted. "Terror is one of the forms of military action that may be perfectly suitable and even essential at a definite juncture in the battle, given a definite state of the troops and the existence of definite conditions." Lenin did, however, emphatically reject use of terror "as an independent form of occasional attack unrelated to any army." To be effective terror had to be part of a comprehensive strategy for gaining power. Such a strategy could only be devised and implemented by a revolutionary organization. In the absence of such an organization, individual acts of terror, no matter how heroic and dramatic, could be counterproductive, diverting energy away from the task of building the organization and bringing repression down upon a fragile revolutionary movement.[5]

Anti-Colonial Insurgency

Had he lived to see them, Lenin would certainly have approved the use of terror in "wars of national liberation." This term applies to a series of insurgencies fought to gain independence from colonial rule following World War II. While all of these movements had an ethnic nationalist dimension, only a small number of them embraced communism. Whatever ideology motivated the insurgents, however, they employed the same methods to accomplish their goals: propaganda, guerrilla warfare, and terror. In the vast majority of cases the insurgents succeeded against European powers severely weakened by six years of world war.

Communist ideology did play a major role in two immediate postwar insurgent victories. In Yugoslavia, a new nation created in 1919 by adding Austro-Hungarian territory to the Kingdom of Serbia, Josef Brotz Tito filled the power vacuum created by retreating Axis armies. Tito's communist partisans had fought German and Italian troops and Serb royalist partisans led by Draža Mihailović, whom he defeated in a struggle for control of postwar Yugoslavia. In 1949 Mao Tse-Tung seized control of China using his own brand of communist insurgency, known as "People's War," in which he blended Marxist Leninism with the writings of Chinese philosopher Sun Tzu. Mao developed a phased approach to insurgency beginning with political mobilization and moving through guerrilla warfare to mobile conventional war. While his principle work, *On Guerrilla Warfare*, does not promote use of terror, his other writings and the course of the Chinese revolution demonstrate that he did not oppose its selective use. "To put it bluntly," he proclaimed in a 1927 report on a peasant revolt, "it is necessary to create terror for a while in every rural area, or otherwise it would be impossible to suppress the activities of the counter-revolutionaries in the countryside or overthrow the authority of the gentry." In what has long been the ideologue's rationalization for virtually any excess, he concluded, "Proper limits have to be exceeded in order to right a wrong, or else the wrong cannot be righted."[6]

Mao's writings and even more so his success inspired other insurgents. Ho Chi Minh led his communist Viet Minh in a successful campaign to liberate French Indochina. In addition to conducting guerrilla operations against French troops, he used terror to hold the support of rural hamlets by assassinating local leaders. In 1954 Ho decisively defeated the French at Dien Ben Phu. That defeat led to French withdrawal from Indochina, which the Geneva Accords divided into communist North and democratic South Vietnam. Seeing the Viet Minh victory as the inexorable spread of communism instead of as the anti-colonial war that it also was, the United States embarked upon a long, costly, and demoralizing war, which ended with American withdrawal in 1973 and the unification of Vietnam under communist rule in 1975.[7]

Rather than learn from the failure of Indochina, the French repeated it with even more disastrous consequences in Algeria. A bitter eight-year insurgency (1954–62) witnessed atrocities perpetrated by the insurgent *Front de Libération Nationale*, the colonists known as *Pieds Noirs* (black feet), and the French security forces. Determined, after the loss of Southeast Asia, not to trust the survival of Western Civilization to temporary occupants of the Elysée Palace (i.e., French presidents), the army developed a *guerre révolutionnaire* doctrine of counterinsurgency. During the Battle of Algiers, the Colonial Paratroopers constructed an *"organogram,"* or outline, of the insurgent order of battle. Although they succeeded in neutralizing much of the Front de Libération Nationale organization in the city, their use of torture to gain information alienated support for the struggle among the French people and in the international community.[8]

Insurgents repeated the pattern of Algeria and Indochina throughout the European empires. The British alone enjoyed any success in combating these wars of national liberation. From 1948 to 1960, they faced a communist insurgency in Malaya. Concentrated in the minority Chinese population, the insurgents set up operational bases in remote jungles and linked them to support cells within squatter settlements along the jungle fringe. The insurgents attacked local police, government officials, and small British army units. They terrorized the general population, murdering Malay rubber plantation owners and Chinese rubber tappers who refused to support them. Unlike other revolutionaries, however, the insurgents did not enjoy safe havens and secure sources of supply in a neighboring state. In contrast to the French, the British employed a highly successful counterinsurgency strategy aimed at winning hearts and minds through much needed reform (economic, political and social) with limited and focused use of force. Their methods produced one of the few truly successful counterinsurgency campaigns of the Cold War era.[9]

Although the British repeated the Malayan success in Cyprus (1954–59), Kenya (1952–57), and Oman (1970–75), campaigns did not always run smoothly. The *Mau Mau* insurgency in Kenya turned out to be one of the ugliest episodes in the era of decolonization. The "Land and Freedom" movement, consisting largely of disadvantaged young men from the Kikuyu people, set up camps in the forest from which they sallied forth to murder white farmers and members of their own ethnic group. The security forces, most notably the Kikuyu Home Guard and the Kenya Regiment (consisting largely of white Afrikaners) conducted brutal reprisals and made liberal use of torture.[10] The deplorable conflict cost a minimum of 11,000 lives, including 1,000 hanged by the British in what now seems little more than judicial murder.[11] However, even the insurgents acknowledged that the regular British army committed few of the atrocities. Britain escaped the popular backlash and international criticism that fell upon the French in Algeria because the Mau Mau insurgency remained confined to the Kikuyu, the insurgents' own brutality won them little sympathy, and most atrocities did not come to light until years after the conflict had ended.

Despite its general success, Britain also experienced a major defeat, not at the hands of communist revolutionaries but by ethnic-nationalist insurgents. The Zionist movement in Palestine turned violent in the immediate aftermath of World War II. As large numbers of Holocaust survivors entered the British Mandate of Palestine, the *Irgun Zwei Lumi* launched an insurgency against the colonial government. In 1945 this radical group formed a temporary alliance, the United Resistance Movement, with the officially sanctioned Jewish Agency and its paramilitary *Haganah*, and a third group, *Lochmei Heruth Israel*, a small radical group more commonly know as the "Stern Gang" for its founding member Avrim Stern.[12] Although the insurgents generally confined themselves to guerrilla operations against British forces and infrastructure, they perpetrated what at the time many considered the worst terrorist attack to date. On July 22, 1945, the Irgun bombed the King David Hotel in Jerusalem. The British either ignored a warning to evacuate the building or received it too late, perhaps both. The attack killed 92 people and injured 69 others.[13] Although the hotel housed British Headquarters and could be seen as a legitimate target, innocent civilians lost their lives. The incident caused the break up of the United Resistance Movement.[14] Still, the insurgency persisted until the British, seeing no benefit worth the cost of remaining in Palestine, tossed the problem to the United Nations (successor to the League of Nations, which had created the British Mandate of Palestine) like a hot potato.

The ensuing declaration of Israeli independence and subsequent Arab-Israeli War led to use of terror on both sides. One of the more infamous incidents occurred at the village of Dayr Yasin, where the Irgun together with the Stern Gang massacred 115 men, women and children, stuffing their mutilated bodies down wells. In retaliation, Arab fighters murdered 70 Jewish doctors and nurses in a convoy headed for Jerusalem.[15]

The struggle for Palestine illustrates several important points about insurgency and terrorism. The displacement of hundreds of thousands of Palestinians as a result of the conflict set in motion events that have fueled insurgency and terrorism ever since. Terrorist incidents have both immediate and very long-term consequences. The conflict also demonstrates that urban insurgency is far more challenging than its rural counterpart, a lesson reinforced by the British withdrawal from Aden in 1967 and the thirty-year struggle in Northern Ireland. The insurgency in Iraq confirms the lesson once more.

Other Insurgencies

Inspired by the success of anti-colonial wars, ethnic nationalist movements continued to spawn insurgent groups. Insurgent victories over "soft" colonial targets in Africa and Asia led analyst J. Bowyer Bell to refute what he called the "the myth of the guerrilla"—an unshakable faith in the irresistible nature of insurgent warfare.[16] A separatist movement demanded an independent state consisting of Basque Provinces in Spain and France. The Basque separatist organization ETA launched a campaign of violence in the 1960s. ETA received support from a Basque population deprived of its language, culture, and institutions by the dictatorship of Francisco Franco and sympathy from many Spaniards unhappy with the dictatorship. ETA attacked police and government institutions within the Basque region itself and in the Spanish capital Madrid. In 1973, ETA achieved a stunning success by assassinating Admiral Luis Carrero Blanco, Franco's handpicked successor. Blanco's status as a military man and top official of an authoritarian regime arguably made him the legitimate target of what was a military operation not a terrorist attack.

The insurgents' greatest achievement also began its decline. Following Franco's death in 1975, democracy returned to Spain. A new constitution (1978) granted the Basque region limited autonomy, legitimized use of the Basque language, and restored local institutions. Despite these concessions, ETA continued its campaign of violence, launching its most intense wave of attacks after the democratic process had gotten under way.[17] In 1980 alone, ETA killed 76 people, the largest annual death rate in its history.[18] That year may be the point at which ETA ceased being an insurgency working for legitimate political goals and became a mere terrorist organization devoted to violence in the service of an unattainable utopian dream. The pattern of attacks confirms this change: ETA had previously targeted police, military, and government officials; it now attacked innocent civilians. In 1987, the terrorists detonated a bomb in a Barcelona shopping mall killing 21 people. Spaniards who had once privately cheered the assassination of Admiral Carrero Blanco turned out in droves to protest this senseless act of murder.

The ETA campaign of the 1980s spawned a counter-campaign of state terror. A right-wing terrorist organization called the Anti-Terrorist Liberation Group (GAL, from the initials of its Spanish name, *Grupo Antiterrorista de Liberación*) assassinated suspected terrorists in the Spanish and French Basque regions, killing 27 people in 25 attacks.[19] GAL, one of several such groups, turned out to be sponsored by the Spanish Interior Ministry.[20] Although the GAL death squads drew widespread criticism, they may have encouraged France to abandon its policy of tacitly allowing ETA to operate within its territory. Paris and Madrid signed an extradition treaty depriving ETA of its safe haven in Basque territory across the

Pyrenees. They later agreed to allow hot pursuit of suspects by French and Spanish police 60 kilometers on either side of the border. Within Spain a government crackdown reduced the organization's effectiveness. ETA declared a ceasefire in 1998, and many considered the organization finished. However, the organization resumed its terrorist campaign in 2000, conducting sporadic murders during the next six years. Having gained nothing from these senseless murders, ETA declared a permanent ceasefire in March 2006.

As the ETA campaign unfolded in Spain, popular discontent in Northern Ireland erupted into a violent insurgency that would last three decades and take over 3,000 lives. For the half century since the partition of Ireland into an independent state and a British province, Catholics in the North had lived under an apartheid regime, exposed to systematic discrimination in all areas of life and frequent intimidation from the police if they objected to their treatment. Under-represented because of electoral gerrymandering, denied equal opportunity in housing, employment, and education, the Catholic community initially chose nonviolent protest in the vein of Martin Luther King Jr. Police brutality and Protestant intransigence led to widespread sectarian violence in the summer and fall of 1969. The British government sent in the army to stop the rioting but also to protect the Catholic community. They then made two fateful decisions in the aftermath of the riots: they disarmed the Royal Ulster Constabulary and declared certain Catholic neighborhoods "no-go areas," in the hope that pulling the security forces back would calm the situation. Into this security vacuum, however, stepped the Provisional Irish Republican Army (PIRA), which gained control of Catholic neighborhoods and launched a systematic campaign of terror that would last thirty years.[21] At first PIRA attacked police and British soldiers in the province, but then they expanded their attacks to the British mainland and even targeted the United Kingdom's North Atlantic Treaty Organization (NATO) forces on the continent. Protestant paramilitary groups launched a terrorist campaign of their own against the Catholic community. Both PIRA and its Protestant counterparts (such as the Ulster Volunteer Force) used enforcement terror against their own communities. From 1969 to 1999, 3,744 people died in the conflict, 2,038 of them innocent civilians.[22] Despite a slow start and serious blunders, including the Bloody Sunday massacre (1972), the British security forces developed an effective counterinsurgency strategy based on past experience adapted to new circumstances. By the early 1990s the British security forces had achieved stalemate with PIRA and demonstrated that they could not be forced out of Northern Ireland. This realization and a vastly changed post-Cold-War world encouraged the insurgents to seek a peaceful political solution to the conflict. PIRA agreed to a cease-fire in 1994 and in 1998 signed the Good Friday Accords, a complex agreement that required power sharing in Northern Ireland while providing a role for both the British and Irish governments in the governance of the province. In July 2005, PIRA announced that it would decommission its weapons. Much remains to be done to build a working government and a sustainable pluralistic society, but the likelihood of renewed violence seems remote.

In addition to conducting a counterinsurgency campaign in Northern Ireland, Britain assisted the government of Oman in combating an insurgency in Dhofar province from 1970 to 1975. Operating from across the border in South Yemen, communist insurgents fomented rebellion against the Sultan of Oman's government. The British seconded (loaned) 150 officers to the Sultan's armed forces, and another 300 privately contracted with the Omani government. This leaven of talented and experienced soldiers reinforced by units from Britain's elite special forces, the Special Air Service (SAS), turned the tide of the conflict. Following a coup to replace the aging Sultan with his more progressive son, the British and Omanis developed a comprehensive strategy to defeat the insurgents concentrated on the Jebel plateau. To win back the disaffected population they created Civil Action Teams responsible for building schools, clinics, and mosques, drilled wells and provided veterinary care for livestock. An information warfare campaign used Islam to combat God-less communism. Small local militia units known as *Firqats* (Arabic for "fighters") trained and led by SAS teams defended their villages and gathered intelligence on the insurgents. These measures and a series of offensive drives anchored on fortified lines across the plateau defeated the insurgency.[23]

A more intractable ethnic separatist insurgency has plagued the small Asian Nation of Sri Lanka since the mid 1970s. Created in 1972 the Liberation Tigers of Tamil-Eelam have fought for an independent Tamil state in the northern and eastern areas of Sri Lanka, where most of the Tamil minority (18% of the population) lives. It carried out its first terrorist act with the murder of the mayor of Jaffna in 1975 and began a systematic campaign of terror in 1977. The insurgents formed an army and "liberated" the Tamil area of the north, establishing their own government there. Like other insurgents, they have employed terror against Sri Lankan security forces, government officials, and Tamil leaders who oppose them. Unlike most insurgents they have also targeted the Singhalese population by bombing an airplane, bus stations, and a political rally. They have also conducted high profile assassinations, most notably Indian Prime Minister Rajiv Gandhi in 1991 (in retaliation for Indian intervention against them), the Sri Lankan defense minister in the same year, and the Sri Lankan President in 1993. The Sri Lankan armed forces have contained the insurgents, who declared a ceasefire in 2001 and abandoned their demand for independence in favor of a call for local autonomy. Violence erupted again in 2006 and resolution of the conflict remains illusive.[24]

Insurgencies against unpopular governments also took place in Latin America during this period. In 1960 Nicaraguan exiles formed a National Liberation Front to overthrow the dictatorial regime of the Samosa family in power since the 1930s. Two years later the insurgents decided to honor the revolutionary leader Augusto César Sandino by changing the group's name to Sandinista National Liberation Front. The movement enjoyed little success until the late 1970s, when it fractured into three parts, one of which adopted more aggressive tactics and seized power in 1979. Although the Sandinistas did perpetrate some terrorist acts, they enjoyed considerable popular support, evidenced by their ability to defeat an army of 14,000 with only 1,500 guerrillas.[25] The Sandinista victory did not, however, end the violence. Concerned about the spread of communism in the Western Hemisphere, President Ronald Reagan supported a covert war led by Nicaraguan Contras operating out of neighboring Guatemala. While they did attack Salvadoran Army units, the Contras also waged a brutal campaign of terror against Salvadoran civilians. The Contra war combined with international pressure forced free elections that ousted the Sandinistas in 1990. They retained some paramilitary capability, continued to contest elections, and conducted sporadic acts of terrorism throughout the 1990s. A return to the violence of the past, however, seems very unlikely.

In El Salvador the *Farabundo Mariti National Liberation Front* (FMLN), an alliance of five resistance groups, launched an insurgency against the repressive government in San Salvador. The Marxist FMLN attracted widespread support amongst urban and rural poor in a country in which 15 families controlled approximately 90% of the wealth. The insurgency developed into a full-blown civil war with the FMLN controlling considerable Salvadoran territory. Although both sides used terror, government forces and right-wing paramilitary death squads committed the worst atrocities. They murdered priests and assassinated Archbishop Oscar Romero of San Salvador, who spoke out against government abuses but never endorsed the FMLN, and five Jesuit priests at the University of Central America in 1989. The army, however, committed the worst atrocity, massacring almost all of the inhabitants of the village of El Mazote in 1981. As their momentum ground to a halt, the FMLN too murdered innocent civilians, tossing hand grenades onto buses in San Salvador. A 1991 cease-fire led to a negotiated settlement that included reform and turned the FMLN into a legitimate political party.

During the 1980s Peru faced a concerted rural insurgency launched by *Sendero Luminoso* (Shining Path). Founded in 1969 by Manuel Rubén Abimael Guzman Reynoso, the organization adopted a Maoist strategy of drowning the cities in a sea of peasants. Guzman exploited rural poverty and resentment by Peru's native Indian population, who had suffered discrimination since the Spanish conquest of the sixteenth century.

He built his support base for a decade before formally declaring war on the government in 1980. Shinning Path focused its campaign of terror on civilian officials in the countryside in order to break the link with the state and gain support through demonstrating government weakness.[26] An inappropriate government response relying on the overuse of conventional force helped the insurgency spread. In the early 1990s a new strategy based on British counterinsurgency yielded better results.[27] The government exploited Shining Path's one fatal weakness, reliance on a single charismatic leader. The capture of Guzman in 1992 dealt the organization a near fatal blow, but the government failed to exploit its advantage in part because of its need to deploy troops to the Ecuadorian border. Resolution of the international dispute in 1995 allowed the government to redeploy troops against the insurgents, whom they defeated with the capture of Shinning Path's last major leader in 1999.[28]

While Shining Path enjoyed success in the countryside, another insurgent movement developed in the cities. The Túpac Amaru Revolutionary Movement (MRTA, from its Spanish name, *Movimiento Revolucionario Túpac Amaru*) formed in 1983 and began operations the following year. Despite its commitment to Marxist ideology, MRTA never attracted enough support to move beyond the level of mere terrorism. Its greatest success proved its downfall. In December 1996 MRTA seized the Japanese embassy in Lima taking over 400 hostages and launching a four-month standoff. An assault by Peruvian security forces in April freed the remaining hostages and killed all of the terrorists, including many top MRTA leaders, permanently crippling the organization.[29]

Colombia has faced the most tenacious, persistent and intractable insurgent challenge in history. In a country with great social inequities and a long history of internal conflict, Marxism found fertile ground. In the late 1950s a number of groups coalesced into FARC. The group, which aims to establish a Marxist state, has engaged in guerrilla warfare and terrorism over the past forty years. To fund its activities FARC engages in kidnapping and narcotics trafficking. The organization has become so involved in the production and sale of cocaine that it has arguably become less an insurgent group and more a drug cartel. FARC controls an entire province whose main industry is coca production. With an estimated strength of 9,000 to 12,000 members, the organization has little prospect of seizing power but neither can it be easily defeated.[30] In addition to FARC, the Colombian government faces other terrorist groups, organized criminals, and right-wing, paramilitary death squads.

While other South American countries faced terrorism perpetrated by self-proclaimed revolutionary organizations, these groups never rose to the level of insurgencies. The governments of Argentina, and to a lesser extent Uruguay, dealt with terrorist threats through draconian measures that constituted state terrorism. The military junta that ruled Argentina and conducted the Dirty War against political opponents in the 1970s behaved far worse than any terrorist group it opposed.

Ideological Terrorism in Europe

While insurgents used terror as one tactic in a broad strategy to seize power, others used it to promote broad ideological agendas without attainable political goals. A waive of such terror swept Europe during the 1960s, perpetrated by a generation of disillusioned middle class youth. In Germany the Red Army Faction (RAF), better known as the Baader-Meinhof Gang for its two colorful leaders (Andreas Baader and Ulrike Meinhof), launched a terrorist campaign based on Marxism and committed to ridding Germany of perceived Nazi influences. The RAF assassinated industrial leaders, bombed buildings, and perpetrated bank robberies. Sympathetic to the Palestinian cause, the group collaborated with the Popular Front for the Liberation of Palestine to hijack an Air France flight to Entebbe Airport in Uganda in 1976. With its abstract ideology and broad, diffuse goals, the movement failed to attract enough new followers to stay in business. The RAF suffered a serious setback with the death of Baader in 1977, but continued sporadic attacks until 1991. With most of its leaders dead or in prison the RAF officially dissolved itself in 1998.

The Red Brigades followed the pattern of Baader-Meinhof, racking Italy with a campaign of bombings and assassinations in the 1970s. For both groups terror became not a means to an end but an end in itself. With little real prospect of success, which they could hardly even define, attacks seemed to validate a heroic if hopeless struggle. At first the Italian government responded halfheartedly to the terrorists, who seemed less of a threat than the country's perennial problem with organized crime. Their attitude changed dramatically with the abduction and murder of former Prime Minister Aldo Moro in 1978. The heinous act outraged the Italian people and raised the Red Brigades from a nuisance to a serious concern. The assassination prodded the government into decisive action. A concerted counterterrorism campaign by the *Caribonarie*, Italy's elite paramilitary police, led to a series of arrests that left the organization shattered by 1982.

The Dutch faced a brief but intense episode of terrorism in 1977, when South Moluccan immigrants living in the Netherlands launched a campaign to prevent annexation of their homeland by Indonesia, a former Dutch colony. They wished to publicize their cause and seemed to have believed, rather oddly, that the Netherlands could still influence events in the East Indies. The campaign reached a climax in June when terrorists seized a Dutch commuter train and a school. One Dutch Royal Marine commando unit stormed the train, killing all six terrorists and freeing the hostages, while another liberated the school, freed the hostages, and captured the terrorists without loss of life.

Greece has also faced a series of terrorist attacks, most perpetrated by domestic groups entwined in the country's complex politics. Two organizations, the 17 November Group and the Revolutionary People's Struggle have operated since the 1970s. Initially formed to oppose Greece's military junta, the groups have since tried to force the Greek government out of NATO and NATO forces out of Greece. 17 November became a concern in May 2004 when it conducted an attack on the eve of the Summer Olympics in Athens. Fortunately, the event turned out to be an isolated incident.

Greece's NATO ally and sometime adversary Turkey has faced considerably more terrorism than other European nations. By far its greatest threat comes from the Kurdistan Workers Party (PKK), a Marxist ethnic separatist movement seeking independence for the Kurdish region of southeastern Turkey and its eventual union with adjoining Kurdish regions in Syria, Iran, and Iraq. Formed in 1974, PKK has conducted an insurgent campaign in Kurdish areas and terrorist attacks throughout Turkey and against Turkish targets abroad. The Turks have long maintained that some European governments turn a blind eye to PKK activities on their soil and accuse Greece of actually abetting the organization. Islamist extremist groups with possible links to al-Qaeda compound Turkey's security concerns. In 2003 one or more of these groups launched a horrific series of attacks in Istanbul, bombing two synagogues on November 15 and a bank and the British consulate five days later.

Since the early 1990s the Russian Federation has faced an insurgency in one of its Muslim republics. A badly handled counterinsurgency campaign to prevent the secession of Chechnya in the north Caucasus turned a local insurgency into an international terrorist problem. Facing a brutal campaign in which the Russians used state terror against the Chechen people, local insurgents formed ties with al-Qaeda. Terrorists operating in the name of the Chechen rebels expanded the conflict with attacks on apartment buildings in neighboring Dagestan and Moscow (1999), a Moscow theater (2002), and a school in Beslan, North Osetia (2004). In both the theater and school attacks the terrorists took hostages, scores of whom died in botched rescue attempts. The cell that struck the theater included non-Chechen members confirming that the rebels were receiving support from other terrorist groups.

Middle East Terrorism

Terrorist groups often defy easy classification, but those in the Middle East are particularly difficult to pin down. Several hybrid groups formed to oppose the creation of Israel and its subsequent occupation of the West Bank and Gaza. These groups have often had some insurgent and some terrorist characteristics, combining political with ideological, and/or religious agendas, and they have evolved over time. A few deserve greater attention than others. Founded in 1959, Yasser Arafat's *Fatah* (an Arabic acronym for "Palestinian National Liberation Movement") carried out attacks against Israel from the West Bank (then part of Jordan) during the early 1960s. Following Israeli occupation of the territory during the Six-Day War in 1967, Arafat moved to Jordan, from there to Lebanon, and finally to Tunisia, each of which served as a base for terrorist activities. In 1974 Arafat gained control of the Palestine Liberation Organization (PLO), an umbrella under which groups like the Popular Front for the Liberation of Palestine, the Palestine Liberation Front, and his own Fatah movement gathered.

Other organizations developed out of the struggle between Israel and the Palestinians. In an effort to rout the PLO out of Lebanon, the Israeli Defense Forces invaded the country in 1982. Operation Peace of Galilee forced Arafat to leave for Tunisia, but it also gave rise to another even more militant organization, the Shiite Hezbollah group supported by Iran. Hezbollah attacked Israeli forces in Southern Lebanon and northern Israel, contributing ultimately to Israeli withdrawal from Lebanon in 2000 and return in June 2006 to stop rocket attacks into northern Israel. An even more troubling organization arose in the occupied territories themselves. In 1987 demonstrations marking the twentieth anniversary of the Israeli occupation of the West Bank an Gaza turned violent and gave birth to *Hamas*, an Arabic acronym for "Islamic Resistance Movement." Even after Yasser Arafat reached an accord with Israeli Prime Minister Yitzak Rabin that created the Palestinian Authority to govern the territories, Hamas refused to recognize Israel's right to exist. With the assassination of Rabin and subsequent collapse of the peace process, Hamas resumed its terrorist campaign, joined by Palestinian Islamic Jihad and the Al Aqsa Martyr's Brigade.

Without necessarily endorsing its use of terror, many Palestinians consider Hamas a legitimate resistance movement struggling to end an illegal occupation. The Israeli government still considers it a mere terrorist organization as does the United States and the European Union. Nonetheless, Hamas fielded candidates in the January 2006 parliamentary elections and won a majority of seats in the Palestinian Legislative Council. Although the party declared a cease-fire and formed a government, Israel and its allies cut off its funds and refuse to deal with Hamas until the group recognizes Israel's right to exist and renounces violence.

Zionism has also spawned its share of terrorist organizations. The Jewish Defense League founded by Rabbi Meir Kahane in 1968 conducted over 30 terrorist attacks against alleged anti-Semites in the United States. In 1971 Kahane emigrated with his family to Israel, where he set up the ultra-conservative Kach party. Kach has perpetrated or encouraged terrorist attacks and vigilante violence against Palestinians in the occupied territories, including the 1983 attack on an Islamic school in Hebron and the 1994 massacre of 29 Muslims praying at Hebron's Cave of the Patriarchs Mosque. A year later another extremist murdered Yitzak Rabin, Prime Minister of Israel, because he had reached a peace accord with the Arabs. In justifying the murder of Rabin, the assassin Yigal Amir explained: "The minute a Jew betrays his people and country to the enemy, he must be killed."[31] Baruch Goldstein, perpetrator of the Hebron massacre, believed his act would secure Israel's possession of the Promised Land and hasten the coming of the Messiah. Both Amir and Goldstein drew inspiration from Meir Kahane's *Gush Emunium* (bloc of the faithful) movement, which wished to expel the Palestinians and make Israel a theocratic state.[32] Israeli security forces foiled an effort by Kahane's followers to blow up the Dome of the Rock (Mosque of Omar) atop Jerusalem's temple mount, the third holiest site in Islam.

Although rarely an intentional target of Middle East terrorist groups, Europeans have suffered attacks by these groups carried out in Europe. The most notorious of these occurred during the 1972 Summer Olympic Games in Munich, West Germany. Members of Black September, a Fatah strike group (named for the 1971 Jordanian attack on Palestinians in that country) kidnapped 11 Israeli athletes, all of whom died in a failed rescue attempt by West German security forces. In 1985 another Palestinian terrorist organization, the Abu Nidal Group, launched simultaneous attacks on the ticket counters of Israel's El Al airline at the Rome and Vienna airports. Libyan dictator Muammar Qaddafi appears to have masterminded or at least supported the April 1986 bombing of a Berlin discotheque and the destruction of Pan Am Flight 103 over Lockerbie, Scotland in December 1988. Two-hundred seventy-seven people died in the attack, 11 of them British subjects killed on the ground. The attack may have been in response to the accidental downing of an Iranian airbus by a U.S. warship in the Persian Gulf.

Unlike Germany, which served as a convenient location for terrorists to attack foreigners on its soil, France has suffered direct attacks by groups involved in the Algerian civil war. In December 1994 the *Groupe Islamique Armée* (GIA, Armed Islamic Group) hijacked an Air France flight en route from Algiers to Paris, intending to crash it into the Eiffel Tower. French Commandos stormed the plane, freeing the hostages and preventing the attack. The Armed Islamic Group also perpetrated a series of bombings in France over the next few years until a crack down on the organization in preparation for France's hosting the 1998 soccer World Cup crippled the organization.

Terrorism in the United States

Although the United States has a long history of terrorist organizations, no domestic group has ever posed a serious threat to national security. Besides the anarchists already discussed, a series of extremists groups have used terror for political or ideological goals. Since the 1960s, groups such as the Black Panthers, Students for a Democratic Society, Armed Revolutionary Movement of Puerto Rico, and the Animal Liberation Front have used violence to further their causes. Most did little more than damage property and stage robberies, a few committed murder, and all could be easily handled by U.S. law enforcement. The anti-abortion movement has also led to terrorism. While most attacks targeted facilities during off hours, some extremists have murdered doctors for performing abortions. During the last decade white supremacist groups, heirs to the Ku Klux Klan, espoused the belief that America should revert to the Aryan Christian nation they assert it had once been. Many groups under the broad umbrella of the Christian Identity Movement claim that they arm themselves only in self-defense and in preparation for the predicted war with the Federal Government or/and the United Nations, which many believe will try to take away their freedom. Some, however, go further, advocating violence without breaking the law by inciting it. Timothy McVeigh and Terry Nichols, the two men who bombed the Murrah Federal Building in Oklahoma City (1995) subscribed to this ideology. During the 1990s some Christian Identity groups armed themselves and formed rural communes to await the imminent return of the Messiah.[33]

The Oklahoma City bombing notwithstanding, so far right-wing extremism has posed more of a potential than an actual threat to national security. Law enforcement, aided by watchdog groups like the Anti-Defamation League and the Southern Law Poverty Institute, monitors hate groups and their activities to make certain that they stay within the law or at least below a certain threshold of behavior. Moving against them prematurely could backfire, provoking them to violence, increasing the support they enjoy in some areas, and driving them deeper underground where monitoring them would be more difficult.

Religious Terrorism

The Christian Identity Movement may also be categorized as "religious terrorism." Some of the Middle East groups, Muslim and Jewish, could also be place in this category along with others that might be considered cults. Japan's Aum Shinrikyo (Aum supreme truth) combined Buddhist, Hindu, and Christian ideas into a belief system that attracted thousands of followers. The group also embraced millenarian terrorism. After several failed attempts to conduct an attack using sarin gas, Aum released the deadly nerve agent in a Tokyo subway in 1995, killing 12 and injuring 1000.[34] The subsequent arrest of the cult leader seems to have diminished its effectiveness. The Lord's Resistance Army in Uganda could also be described as a cult that uses terror.

Terrorism in the name of radical Islam, of course, concerns ordinary people the most. In recent years most of these attacks have been perpetrated by al-Qaeda (and its affiliates), an organization that will be discussed more fully in Chapter 4.

Conclusion

Far from being a new phenomenon, terror has been employed by a variety of actors for a very long time. States have used it for centuries to maintain order and discourage rebellion. Beginning with the anarchists in the second half of the nineteenth century, illegal organizations began to use terror to achieve political goals. Insurgents made limited uses of the weapon as part of a strategy to seize power. Some of them actually succeeded. Other groups have used terror more extensively to achieve broad ideological goals so utopian as to be unattainable. The term "terrorism" most aptly applies to these ideological groups. To be truly useful a historical survey of terrorist activity must be analyzed to reveal trends and patterns.

CHAPTER 3

Patterns and Trends

Prevailing Myths

As the preceding chapter illustrates, terror is a weapon that can be used by state and non-state actors. If the history of terror, or the history of anything for that matter, is to be more than what Henry Ford called "one damn thing after another," some effort must be made to discern trends and patterns over time. Unfortunately, in the post-9/11 world glib assumptions widely circulated and popularly believed have replaced thoughtful analysis, even in some academic circles. The public generally perceives that terrorism has become much more prevalent and far deadlier in recent decades. They see this trend continuing for the foreseeable future and feel helpless to do much about it. They also consider international terrorism a new phenomenon. Each of these assumptions needs further consideration.

Cycles of Violence

Even a cursory examination of terrorist incidents over the past century and a half reveals two inescapable truths: first, terrorism is a perennial problem and second, the frequency of terrorist attacks ebbs and flows. The post–World War II period experienced an upsurge in attacks as have the years since 1990. The level of terrorist activity results from a complex interplay of individual, group, state, and international forces.[1] The weakness of European imperial powers after World War II and the spread of revolutionary ideology encouraged anti-colonial insurgencies that used terror as weapon in those struggles. The current cycle of violence developed in large measure out of trends within the Islamic world but also owes much to the turbulence caused by the end of the Cold War. Greater resources and new technologies have also contributed to the increase in terrorism of recent years. Recognizing that some periods experience more terrorist activity than others, analysts have tried to define clear historical patterns of terrorism. Political scientist David Rapoport, who has studied the phenomenon for over forty years, argues that modern terrorism has unfolded in four distinct waves: the anarchist wave, the anti-colonial wave, the ideological wave, and the religious wave.

The "anarchist wave" began in the late nineteenth century and continued until around 1920. "Modern terrorism," Rapoport asserts, "began in Russia during the 1880s."[2] Marked by dramatic but largely ineffectual assassinations, this period saw the development of clearly defined arguments for the use of terror as a revolutionary weapon. The second, "colonial wave" of terror began around 1920 and ran through the 1960s. During this period, anti-colonial insurgents employed terror as one weapon in an arsenal of revolutionary activity. The more selective use of terror in the service of a broader political strategy proved highly effective. The third, "new left wave" began in the late 1960s and continued through the 1980s. The Vietnam War, according to Rapoport, spawned an upsurge in terrorism as groups ranging from the RAF and Red Brigades to PIRA and the PLO opposed neo-colonial control and/or oppressive regimes. Growing internationalism marked this wave as organizations lent one another moral and material support. A fourth or "religious" wave of terrorism began in 1979, the year the Ayatollah Khomeini seized power in Iran, and continues to the present.[3] Although Islam, in Rapoport's theory, lies at the center of the religious wave, Judaism and Christianity have also given rise to terrorist groups.

Although it does identify significant historical patterns, Rapoport's theory has serious problems. To begin with, many groups or movements in his categories fall outside the chronological boundaries of his waves. The ideological terrorists of the 1970s and 1980s behaved very much like nineteenth-century anarchists.[4] They perpetrated dramatic assassinations and robberies but could accomplish little else. The Japanese Red Army, who became guns for hire during the 1970s and 1980s, in fact proclaimed themselves anarchists. A wave of anti-colonial insurgencies did occur between 1945 (not 1920 as Rapoport suggests) and 1970, as Rapoport describes, but insurgency has persisted as a major security problem around the world. Northern Ireland stands as Europe's longest war of the modern era with the ETA campaign a close second. The FMLN insurgency in El Salvador during the 1980s developed into a full fledged civil war. The FARC insurgency in Colombia and the Shining Path campaign in Peru also fall well outside "the second wave." Finally, while the years since 1979 have indeed been marked by a dramatic increase in religiously motivated terrorism, most of this activity falls within a single faith. It can best be understood on its own terms rather than as part of a worldwide, historical wave.

While terrorism may not fall neatly into discernable waves, periods of increased social, economic, and/or political instability have led to increased terrorist violence and will probably continue to do so. Other historical trends in the evolution of terrorism have less to do with motivation and more to do with means. Technology has placed a vast array of new resources at the disposal of terrorists. Telecommunications in particular has knitted the world together more closely, creating a truly global society with all of the problems and possibilities this transformation entails. Illicit organizations, like nations, corporations, and individuals, have been affected by and make use of the Internet, cell phones, and satellite television. These developments have contributed to both the extent and the intensity of terrorist activity.

Frequency and Severity

Popular opinion has it and many scholars concur that terrorism has become increasingly more severe over the past few decades. They attribute this increased lethality to the religious motivation behind contemporary terrorism. Images of the Twin Towers collapsing on 9/11 combined with Osama bin Laden's vitriolic *fatwas* (religious proclamations) make these contentions difficult to refute. As with many popular beliefs, however, these simple impressions obscure a more complex reality. Lack of consensus on a definition of terrorism and the resulting confusion in the data on terrorist incidents make objective analysis difficult. Deciding whether or not terrorism has indeed gotten worse requires weighing three variables: the frequency of terrorist attacks, the severity of each incident, and the cumulative lethality of terrorist campaigns.

The raw data indicates that the total number of terrorist incidents has increased dramatically over the past forty years, the most significant increases occurring in periods 1980–90 and 2000–06 (see Table 3.1).[5] The number of terrorist incidents more than doubled during the first period, rising from 975 for 1968–80 to 2,007 for 1980–90, declined slightly to 1,987 for 1999–2000, then rose dramatically to 5,585 for 2000–06. These raw numbers, however, hide several important patterns. Almost 40% of all attacks between 1968 and 2006 occurred within the context of nationalist-separatist campaigns (i.e., insurgencies) and posed little or no threat to anyone outside the state or region in which each conflict occurred (see Table 3.2). Much of the increase in terrorist activity between

Table 3.1: Terrorist incidents with injuries and fatalities, 1968–2006.

Time period	Number of incidents	Number of injuries	Number of fatalities
1968–80	975	2,637	1,096
1980–90	2,007	6,851	2,718
1990–2000	1,987	7,952	3,726
2000–06	5,585	34,145	16,223
1968–2006	**10,554**	**51,585**	**23,763**

Table 3.2: Terrorist incidents by group classification, 1968–2006.

Time period	Nationalist-Separatist	Religious	Other
1968–80	437	61	477
1980–90	869	201	937
1990–2000	650	293	1,044
2000–06	2,171	1,502	1,912
1968–2006	**4,127**	**2,057**	**4,370**

2000 and 2006 stems from a single event: the U.S. invasion of Iraq. Disaggregating international incidents tied to purely local conflicts (e.g., the murder of British soldiers in Germany by the PIRA) from the total number of international incidents reveals that international terrorism has not increased as much as most people imagine.

The data also reveal the increasing severity of terrorist attacks, although this trend too is misleading. Both the number of injuries and the number of fatalities have risen more or less steadily over the past forty years with a dramatic jump in dead and injured after 2000. From 1968 to 1980, 1,096 people died in terrorist incidents and 2,637 were injured. For the period 1980–90, the death toll more than doubled to 2,718 and the number of injured jumped to 6,851. During the following decade the number of dead and injured rose by just over 1,000 to 3,726 and 7,952, respectively. Since 2000 the figures skyrocketed, once again due primarily to the Iraq war: 34,145 injured and 16,223 dead (see Table 3.1).[6] However, until 9/11 the number of dead and injured from terrorist attacks has been remarkably small relative to the number of incidents, most of which killed very few people. Nationalist-separatist incidents accounted for more than half of the deaths until 1990. During the decade of the 1990s, religiously motivated terrorism became more lethal than insurgent terrorism but only by a third (See Table 3.3). In other words, terror is not much (if any) more likely to kill or injure the average person today than it was forty years ago.

Data on attacks using terror challenge many prevailing myths about terrorism. Terrorism has become neither as pervasive nor as severe as most people imagine. The number of dead and injured before 2000 was quite small, and much of the mayhem occurred in very localized conflicts leaving the vast majority of people, particularly those in the West, untouched by the violence. Popular perceptions about the danger of terrorism have been profoundly shaped by a few high-profile incidents involving mass casualties, most notably 9/11. This gap between perception and reality mirrors similar perceptions about the risks of flying versus the hazards of driving. Statistically, flying has always been safer, but the number of casualties per plane crash and the media coverage such incidents merit makes air travel seem more dangerous than driving.

Table 3.3: Fatalities resulting from terrorist incidents by group classification, 1968–2006.

Time period	Nationalist-Separatist	Religious	Other
1968–80	659	24	413
1980–90	1,582	734	402
1990–2000	1,245	1,886	595
2000–06	5,268	9,175	1,780
1968–2006	**8,754**	**11,819**	**4,051**

The high profile attacks of recent years do highlight another factor to be considered when analyzing terrorist trends and patterns. The intensity of individual attacks has been increasing. Between 1968 and 2006, there have been 22 attacks that killed 101–300 people each. All occurred since 1979, the year religious fanatics seized the Grand Mosque in Mecca. The deadliest attacks in this category include the 1988 bombing of Pan Am 103 (270 dead); the 1998 U.S. Embassy Bombings in Nairobi and Dar es Salaam (292 dead); and the 2004 Madrid Train bombings (191 dead). The five deadliest attacks (300+ fatalities) since 1968 all occurred after 1985 and four of them happened since 1993. The 9/11 attacks, of course, represent the deadliest terrorist event in history.[7]

Though a small percentage of the total, these mass attacks cannot be dismissed as isolated incidents. One analyst has discovered a significant difference in the number, frequency, and severity of attacks inside and outside the economically advanced nations (known as the G7). While the developing nations experienced far more attacks (6,498 as opposed to 590), these attacks were generally less severe than those against the major economic powers. The researcher also noted a greater frequency of attacks against non-G7 members.[8] On the other hand, attacks against Western countries have on average been more destructive. In other words, modern industrialized states are hit far less frequently but suffer much more severe attacks.

The increasing preference for large attacks inflicting mass casualties requires considerable explanation. Most commentators attribute the trend to the rise in religiously motivated terrorism. Religious extremists tend to see the world in black and white and have little difficulty justifying almost any act undertaken in the name of their cause. They have little concern for public opinion outside of their own community and often refuse to accept that anyone is an "innocent civilian." Even if they do regret innocent loss of life, their attitude seems to be "kill them all and let God sort them out." Terrorist data does indeed suggest a connection between religiously motivated terror and high body count. During the 1990s religiously motivated attacks not only comprised the bulk of terrorist incidents but killed more people than those perpetrated by nationalist-separatist movements, reversing the trend of previous decades (see Table 3.3).[9]

While religious fanaticism certainly contributes to the increasing severity of terrorist attacks, such zeal is not new. Historically conflicts motivated by religion or extreme ideology have been bloodier than those fought for more pragmatic reasons. From 1618 to 1648, the Thirty-Years War between Catholics and Protestants so ravaged Germany that for the next century nation-states agreed to keep wars limited and to fight them according to rules that reduced their impact on the general population. The French Revolution, with its mantra of "liberty, equality, fraternity" ended this restraint and added the word "terror" to the political lexicon. The wars of the French Revolution and Napoleon lasted almost 25 bloody years. In contrast the wars of German and Italian unification were short, sharp affairs fought for limited political objectives. The American Civil War had the hallmarks of a religious crusade and produced the casualties to prove it. The First World War exceeded the violence of all previous conflicts but lacked the barbarism of the Second fought just twenty years later. National Socialism became a kind of religion that fueled a race war between Aryan peoples and all others. The dead will never be fully counted.

Terrorism has mimicked another important trend seen in the evolution of conventional war. Although scholars, media critics, and politicians decry Osama bin Laden's failure to make any distinction between combatants and innocent civilians, his behavior conforms to the pattern of increasing lethality discernable in armed conflict from the eighteenth to the twentieth centuries. Since the Napoleonic era wars have become increasingly total, gradually blurring and ultimately erasing the distinction between civilian and soldier. Union General William T. Sherman set an ominous precedent when he announced that he could, "make Georgia howl," and then cut a sixty-mile wide swathe of destruction from Atlanta to the sea. Sherman did not slaughter women and children, but he did make war on the Confederate people, not merely their army. Submarine warfare and the first limited use of strategic bombing cost civilian lives during the First World War, but it took World War II to obliterate the boundary between civilian and military. German bombers deliberately targeted civilians in Warsaw, Rotterdam, and London. British Bomber Command retaliated with attacks on the working class neighborhoods of Berlin. By the end of the war killing civilians had become the norm as epitomized by Dresden, Hiroshima, and Nagasaki, cities with little or no direct military significance. The attackers aimed to break the enemy will to resists in the forlorn hope that people living under dictators could some how compel their leaders to sue for peace. Only the nuclear stalemate between the United States and the Soviet Union forced a return to limited war. As reprehensible as al-Qaeda's actions certainly are, they follow a well established pattern in the history of human conflict.

Contemporary terrorism may have another motive in achieving increasingly large body counts. Those who use terror play to an audience on a worldwide stage created by modern mass communication. Such an audience seems to demand ever more sensational events to pique its interest. Fed a steady diet of mayhem through prime-time programs and the evening news, the viewing public does not shock as easily as it once did. Hundreds of deaths may be needed to produce the same impact once caused by a few dozen. Terrorists may be responding to the same threshold phenomenon driving other media programming: if it bleeds, it leads, and the more it bleeds, the more attention it attracts.

Terror and Globalization

In addition to its increasing lethality, scholars and ordinary people most frequently comment on terrorism's global reach. Illicit organizations no longer confine their activities to one geographic area that they seek to influence or control. They create worldwide networks with support systems in one place, safe havens in another, and operational units in a third. Once again, however, this seemingly new development has a history.

Terrorism has long had an international dimension. The Irish American community supported political activity and even violence in Ireland from the late nineteenth century through the most recent Troubles in Ulster (1969-1998). "One dollar for relief and one dollar for the bomb or the bullet" has long been a fundraising slogan, referring to the dual need to fund an insurgency and care for its victims. During its most recent campaign, PIRA linked up with the Basque separatist group ETA and trained in Libya, which supplied it with Semtex plastic explosive manufactured in Czechoslovakia. Operational units murdered British soldiers in Germany and then retreated into the relatively safe and anonymous streets of Amsterdam. Germany's RAF joined forces with and received aide from Palestinian organizations. Support from the American Jewish community helped the Irgun and Haganah in their struggle with the British. The Liberation Tigers of Tamil and Elam in Sri Lanka receive money raised by their diaspora community abroad.

Terrorist organizations certainly have increased their global reach over the past decade, but the change has been largely a matter of degree. A single technological innovation has promoted internationalism among terrorists as it has among everything else: the Internet. From its modest beginnings in the 1980s, this global network of computers and websites allows people with common interests ranging from coin collecting to terrorism to find each other and share information. By the mid 1990s, 60 million users interacted through 3.2 million host computers linked to 18,000 private and public networks; by the early years of the twenty-first century, the number of users had reached over a billion.[10] People who may lack a steady job, clean drinking water, and adequate healthcare can still go online. Virtually all of the world's 40 active terrorist organizations have at least one website, and some have several in different languages.[11]

Terrorist organizations use the Internet in several ways. They publicize the terrorists' cause, raise money, and recruit members. The worldwide web contains valuable information on targets the terrorists wish to attack, including vulnerabilities and even security measures in place to protect them. The web allows diverse illicit groups with no common goal to exchange information and ideas, including practical information on bombing making.[12] Several active sites contain copies of *The Terrorist Handbook: Explosive Recipes*, which explains in detail how to make different types of bombs from a variety of materials.[13] In at least 30 bombings and 4 attempted bombings in the United States between 1985 and June 1996, the perpetrators had gotten useful information from the Internet.[14] According to Ahmad al-Watheq Billah in an article published on the Global Islamic Media center website, "Al-Qaeda now has a virtual university that teaches electronic jihad."[15] According to one analyst, the Internet rather than a geographic location has become the terrorists' base.[16]

While such observations contain a great deal of truth, they should not be taken too literally. Terrorist attacks are not perpetrated by cyber ghosts traveling invisibly across the airwaves to materialize, strike, and disappear. Real people belonging to specific organizations that need resources attack concrete targets at specific times and places. The Internet facilitates their operations but does not itself cause them. The goals of most terrorist organizations remain predominantly focused on specific regions and countries even while the new technologies allow them to operate further afield. Terrorists now have a global reach but they still have a local agenda even when they see that local agenda as part of a larger movement.

Root Causes

The root causes vary with the type of terrorism. For insurgents, the important question is not why they use terror to support rebellion but why they rebel in the first place. The nineteenth-century revolutionaries tried to replace the existing political system with one better able to meet the needs of ordinary people. They sought to turn social unrest caused by widespread poverty into revolutionary zeal. Poverty alone, however, does not automatically lead to violent upheaval focused on specific political goals. People unhappy with their circumstances must be persuaded that the situation can change and be given guidance as to how best to bring that change about. Revolutionary ideology channels popular discontent in political directions.

The term "popular" has to be qualified. Very few people engaged in the hand-to-mouth struggle to survive have time to consider, never mind devise, revolutionary ideology. A small group of dedicated revolutionaries devise strategies based on the theories of an even smaller group of ideologues. Ironically, both the thinkers and the planners come from well-off families with the resources to educate and support them while they devote their time and energy to politics. The majority of people, perhaps 80% of the population, wish merely to survive or perhaps make their lives a little better. During any revolution, they sit on the fence, becoming active only as necessity dictates and ultimately throwing in their lot with whoever seems likely to win.[17] In 1917 Russian peasants and factory workers rioted not for Marxism but for bread. Lenin focused desperation and anger on political targets. The indifference of most people to ideology explains why revolutionary insurgents keep their use of terror limited. It does not take much to push people back to the side of the government.

Anti-colonial insurgents had a somewhat easier task than social revolutionaries. They often addressed people already enjoying a comfortable standard of living and persuaded them that they should govern their own affairs. Political independence has a broad appeal across the social spectrum, and the use of terror against colonial rulers and those who collaborate with them does not cost the insurgents support among the people who matter most, their own countrymen and women. The insurgents must, however, be careful to avoid killing innocent civilians even by accident. Their use of violence can also cost them the international support often vital to independence movements.

Terror in the service of broad ideological or religious goals has more complex roots. Economic hardship and political disenfranchisement play a role but may not be a sufficient or even primary cause of terrorism. A profound visceral fear that a groups' entire way of life has come under attack seems to motivate much contemporary terrorism. Both the Christian Identity Movement and al-Qaeda explicitly oppose the advance of Western secularism. The Internet and satellite television have done much to promote this fear. The new communications media highlights relative deprivation (the have-nots of the world get to see how much the haves really possess) and disseminates morally objectionable material that cannot easily be censored. The homogenizing effect of globalization threatens to make every place just like every other place, creating social and psychological dissonances that produce violence.[18] Demographic change caused by dramatic population growth or large-scale immigration can have the same result.[19] History, especially when combined with geography, may inspire an ethnic group with a strong belief that it has been treated unjustly or a powerful feeling of loss ("This land is ours," vs.

"That land once belonged to us."), both of which can lead to terrorist violence.[20]

No matter how seriou they may be, grievances alone do not produce terrorism. The same factors that spawn terrorist organizations in one place may give rise to cults in another and street gangs in a third. As with social revolution or anti-colonial insurgency, terrorist ideology integrates discontent and focuses it on a suitable target. Ideology may be secular or religious. Secular ideologies like Marxism often take on the characteristics of religious fanaticism. Religious ideology may be "messianic" (looking to some future hope) or "revivalist" (seeking to restore some real or imagined past). Whatever its precise content, ideology persuades people that a desired end state can be achieved through violent means.

Terrorist Profiles

Identifying root causes of terrorism does not explain why some individuals and not others join a terrorist group. Poverty often leads to crime, sometimes produces violence (individual and communal), but rarely encourages individuals to become terrorists. Root causes explain why groups support terrorist organizations but not why individuals join them. The answer to that question lies not in the disciplines of history and politics but in the field of human psychology. Terrorist recruits often feel alienated from their society and/or frustrated in their ambitions.[21] Some have experienced personal humiliation or witnessed humiliation of those they love, a prominent common experience among Palestinian terrorists.[22] Given the subjective nature of feelings, predicting who will become a terrorist can be difficult. The Baader-Meinhof Group (RAF) provides a clear illustration. Andreas Baader, who dropped out of high school and engaged in petty crime before joining the RAF, seemed to fit the profile of a troubled youth ripe for recruitment by a terrorist group. Ulrike Meinhof, on the other hand, was a university educated journalist with twin daughters enjoying a comfortable middle class life when she became a terrorist and helped Baader escape from prison. Whatever the precise reason, recruits feel powerless and the group empowers them. Whether such individuals become terrorists, gang bangers, or cult members may be merely a matter of opportunity.

One special category of terrorist recruits deserves special consideration because its impact has been so devastating: suicide bombers. Although by no means unique to Middle Eastern terrorism, suicide bombing has achieved its greatest notoriety through the Israeli-Palestinian conflict in which it has been used most extensively—at least until the U.S.-led invasion of Iraq. The perplexing question of why someone volunteers to be a suicide bomber has been the subject of considerable speculation and, fortunately, some solid research that refutes most of the speculation. Nasra Hassan has done extensive work on suicide bombers, interviewing 250 Palestinian extremists, bombers who survived because their bombs failed to detonate, family members of successful bombers, and those who train them. She found that they ranged in age from 18 to 38, came from diverse economic backgrounds (including many who were middle and a few who were upper class), and did not fit the profile of a suicidal person (depression, mental illness, etc.). Their communities considered them model youths and described them as deeply religious. Their families received $3,000–$5,000, but Hassan found no evidence that money motivated the recruits. They felt a strong need to do something about the situation in Palestine, believed that their deaths would really matter, and believed not only that they would be welcomed into paradise for their sacrifice but would be able to intercede on behalf of 70 others on judgment day. They all insisted emphatically that they were not committing suicide, which Islam forbids, but accepting martyrdom.[23]

The process of preparation for martyrdom may be as important as the choice of bombers. Hamas usually rejects those under 18, sole wage earners, only sons, and those with families.[24] Potential recruits go through a careful screening process to confirm their religiosity and commitment. Once selected, recruits undergo a period of intense preparation that includes prayer, directed study of the *Holy Quran*, fasting, and lectures lasting two hours a day. Finally, they make a last will and testament on paper, video, audio cassette, or all three, quoting the *Quran*, explaining their free decision to accept martyrdom, and exhorting others to follow their example. Each bomber repeatedly views his own video testament and those of other martyrs.[25] Hassan's research does not substantiate claims that videos may be used to shame bombers who wish to back out or allegations that a handler follows them with a remote detonator in case they get cold feet. Her interviewees would, of course, be unlikely to share such information even (or especially) if it were true. Iraqi suicide bombers would appear to confirm Hassan's findings, although more research needs to be done on them and on non-Muslim suicide bombers.

Female suicide bombers, a relatively new phenomenon in Middle East terrorism though used previously by the Liberation Tigers of Tamil and Elam in Sri Lanka, differ from their male counterparts in one crucial respect. Besides possessing the requisite religious fervor, they have also experienced some personal trauma. One woman volunteered to be a suicide bomber after she learned that she could not have children. A Chechen woman whose daughter was dying of tuberculosis also agreed to die for the cause. Women may have an advantage over men in that security forces tend to search them less thoroughly.[26]

Conclusion

Beneath the dizzying array of statistics, conflicting theories, and historical patterns lie some basic truths that can make contemporary terrorism clearer and less frightening than it might otherwise be. First, terrorism has been a persistent phenomenon for well over a century. Terrorist activity during this period does not fall neatly into waves or cycles, but it does correlate with political instability, particularly instability that creates power vacuums. Significantly, the collapse of empires at the end of the First World War and the withdrawal of European powers from their colonies after World War II ushered in periods of increased terrorist activity as did the end of the Cold War in 1989 and subsequent collapse of the Soviet Union. In each period the contest for control of the newly created states formed in the wake of imperial withdrawal spawned insurgencies with their accompanying use of terror.

Most of the terror employed by illicit groups has served the larger political goal of gaining power within a particular state or region. Despite widespread belief to the contrary, contemporary terrorists usually promote an agenda with geographically focused goals. Al-Qaeda and its affiliates have always been most concerned with events in the Muslim world. They seek to replace apostate regimes with governments that would rule by *sharia* or Islamic law. As will be seen in the next two chapters, the United States became a target because it supports the Egyptian and Saudi regimes. 9/11 happened not because bin Laden hates the United States, but because the United States has interfered in the Muslim world. Even then the American homeland has suffered only two al-Qaeda attacks in the almost twenty years of the organization's existence: the 1993 World Trade Center bombing and 9/11. Most attacks since then have occurred in Afghanistan and Iraq and should be understood primarily as resistance to foreign occupation.

The pattern of contemporary terrorist activity underscores another important point. The average American is far less likely to be a victim of terrorism than he/she imagines. Television magnifies events and spreads fear as terrorists hope. Individual attacks have become more deadly but remain infrequent. Their intensity has the same effect on the public as an airline crash. Flying has always been much safer than driving, but a few dramatic accidents create the opposite impression.

Frequency of attacks and casualties do not, however, tell the whole story. 9/11 alone inflicted billions of dollars in direct and indirect costs. The demonstrated willingness of terrorists to inflict mass casualties suggests that should they ever acquire a weapon of mass destruction (nuclear, chemical, or biological), they would not hesitate to use it. Even if the United States withdrew entirely from all Muslim countries in which it has a presence, ended its support for Egypt, and cut all ties with

Israel, bin Laden might well continue his attacks on the American homeland and against U.S. targets overseas. Terrorism clearly poses a serious threat to the United States and must be countered. However, it must be countered through rational planning derived from understanding, not from paranoia.

An effective strategy for combating terrorism should attack its root causes. These causes include poverty, rapid demographic change, historic grievances (especially those involving territory), and the destabilizing effects of globalization. Some but not all of these causes can be addressed by the United States and its allies. Dealing with the psychological factors that motivate individuals from disaffected populations to join terrorist organizations as opposed to merely supporting them will be much more difficult. Individuals alienated from their societies have never been in short supply. Suicide bombers, on the other hand, seem to be associated with deeply entrenched conflicts and serve religiously motivated terrorist organizations who offer them more in the afterlife than they can ever hope for in the here and now.

CHAPTER **4**

The al-Qaeda Exception?

Prevailing Myths

When Americans speak of terrorism, they usually mean al-Qaeda. The organization has become for this generation what communism was for their parents and grandparents: a monolithic, evil force inimical to their very way of life. If pressed, most Americans would define al-Qaeda as an organization created by Osama bin Laden to make war on the United States, because, to quote President Bush, he hates "our way of life." That "way of life" may be Christianity, secularism, Western democracy, or any combination of the three. The local political issues motivating bin Laden and those who follow him receive little attention in the United States as does the complex and evolving nature of al-Qaeda. The 9/11 attacks seemed to confirm a popular belief that Islam is an atavistic religion incorrigibly prone to violence.

The decision to dub the struggle against al-Qaeda a "Global War on Terrorism" reflects a Cold-War mentality that sees international affairs as a Manichean contest between good and evil. This popular view echoes the conclusion of some scholars that a broad ideological struggle between worldviews has replaced traditional rivalries between power blocs and alliances. In a 1993 *Foreign Affairs* article and subsequent book renowned political scientist Samuel Huntington argued that "culture and cultural identities . . . are shaping the patterns of cohesion, disintegration, and conflict in the post–Cold War World." Huntington envisioned a major fault line, moved considerably to the East by the demise of the Soviet Union, separating "the peoples of Western Christianity, on the one hand, from Muslim and Orthodox peoples on the other."[1] A decade later Bernard Lewis suggested that Islamic terrorism arose from a collective inferiority complex in the Muslim world over its declining power in the modern world.[2] Unfortunately, both authors encourage the prevailing myth that the world's 1.3 billion Muslims can be viewed monolithically. They also highlight an important truth that ethno-religious identity shapes the consciousness of millions of people, some of whom will become violent when they perceive that identity threatened.

A simplistic view of violence in the name of Islam as an inevitable outgrowth of the religion and the equally naïve treatment of this violence as a mere aberration impede understanding of contemporary terrorism. Al-Qaeda must be understood on several levels. It began as an organization, evolved into a network, and morphed into a broad extremist movement rooted in a major current of contemporary Islam. Understanding al-Qaeda as it has evolved over time also reveals its core goals, which have remained throughout a mixture of concrete political objectives focused in the Middle East and a broad utopian vision of a unified Muslim world governed as a single community or *uma* under Islamic law (*sharia*). A comprehensive picture of al-Qaeda reveals the attraction the movement has for a dedicated corps of fighters and its broader appeal in the Muslim world.

Osama bin Laden the Man

In a few brief years Osama bin Laden has gone from relative obscurity to being the most wanted man on the planet. For all his notoriety as an arch villain, however, the world knows surprisingly little about the man himself. Osama bin Muhammad bin Laden was born on July 30, 1957 in Riyadh, Saudi Arabia, the seventeenth son of Muhammad Awdah bin Laden. The elder bin Laden had emigrated from Yemen to Saudi Arabia where he made a fortune in the construction business and sired 52 children by four wives and numerous concubines. Osama's Syrian mother Hamida raised him in Medina and the surrounding Hijaz region. He attended school in Jeddah, married a Syrian relative of his mother and went on to King Abdulaziz University. He studied economics and management but dropped out during his third year without earning a degree. While at university he fell under the influence of mentors who exposed him to the radical brand of Islam that would shape his life.[3]

Osama bin Laden might have remained in obscurity were it not for the Soviet invasion of Afghanistan in 1979. Incensed by the occupation of an Islamic land by godless communists, bin Laden joined a wave of *mujahedeen*, "holy warriors" from the Arab world who fought alongside the Afghan tribes in a holy war to oust the invaders. As with so much of his life, outsiders know little of bin Laden's activities in Afghanistan. He may have participated in some military actions but probably played no major role in the fighting. He contributed most to the campaign by funding the recruitment, training, and travel to Afghanistan of more mujahedeen. The Service organization he created to facilitate this activity evolved into al-Qaeda.

It would be difficult to exaggerate the impact of the Soviet withdrawal on the morale of bin Laden and the group of mujahedeen known as the

"Afghan Arabs." Victory reinforced the belief that these warriors truly possessed a divine mandate and may even have encouraged their sense of invincibility. Bin Laden not only took credit for the defeat, ignoring American support the mujahedeen received from the United States, but actually exaggerated the significance of the war. In a 1997 interview on CNN he referred to "the collapse of the Soviet Union in which the US has no mentionable role, but rather the credit goes to God, Praise and Glory be to Him, and the mujahedeen in Afghanistan."[4]

After the Soviet withdrawal, bin Laden returned to his native Saudi Arabia. When Saddam Hussein invaded Kuwait in 1990 and threatened the Saudi Kingdom, bin Laden offered the services of his mujahedeen to defend the kingdom. The Royal family declined his offer in favor of support from a coalition led by the United States. Inviting the "crusaders" onto the sacred soil of Saudi Arabia, where once the feet of the Prophet had walked, earned the monarchy bin Laden's undying enmity. From that time forward both the United States and the Saudi regime would become targets, although it would take the United States more than five years to be aware of the threat bin Laden posed.

Following the Gulf War bin Laden left Saudi Arabia for Sudan, which became al-Qaeda's base of operations for the next five years.[5] The Saudis revoked his citizenship and seized his assets in their country in 1994. In 1996, American pressure on Sudan forced him to return to Afghanistan, where he remained until the American invasion following 9/11. He eluded capture during that war and slipped the noose again during an operation to capture him in the Tora Bora Cave region in the spring of 2002. Bin Laden has remained in hiding ever since, and although his precise whereabouts remain unknown, the best intelligence estimates place him along the rugged and uncontrolled southeast border of Afghanistan and Pakistan. What, if any, actual control he now exercises over his organization remains unclear.

Beyond bin Laden the man lies bin Laden the myth. No matter how much the West vilifies him, or perhaps because they do, he remains a folk hero in much of the Muslim world. The headmaster of one of the largest religious schools in Pakistan considers him a "hero because he raised his voice against the outside powers that are trying to crush Islam."[6] Presumably the master's students share this view of bin Laden.

"We love him," a small boy in a remote village in Yemen observed. "He fights for God's sake and he is in Afghanistan."[7] Many Muslims living in the West share this view. An Islamic conference held in London during 2000 praised the al-Qaeda leader as "this man who sacrifices his life for Islam."[8] A 2005 Pew Charitable Trust Global Attitudes survey found that 60% of Jordanians, 51% of Pakistanis, 35% of Indonesians, and 26% of Moroccans have "a lot/some" confidence in bin Laden.[9]

Al-Qaeda the Organization

Al-Qaeda, Arabic for the "the base", began as a simple organization with a single purpose. In 1984 Osama bin Laden and his spiritual mentor Abdullah Azzam founded the *Maktab al Khidmat lil Mujadidin al Arab* ("Afghan Service Bureau") to facilitate recruitment of mujahedeen to fight the Soviets in Afghanistan. As that war drew to a close, the two wished to keep the organization in being to aid other Muslims under threat around the world, and so they created al-Qaeda in 1988, a new organization that drew upon the resources of its more legitimate predecessor.[10] Azzam and Osama disagreed over organization and methods, and a power struggle between the two ended with the assassination of Azzam and his two sons in Peshawar in 1989, probably orchestrated by bin Laden. Now firmly under his control, al-Qaeda would focus on promoting terrorism in defense of Islam.

During the first decade of its existence, al-Qaeda developed into a very hierarchical organization. At the top sat bin Laden himself, surrounded by a *shura* or council of perhaps a dozen members, which in turn supervised five standing committees. The military committee ran training camps and procured weapons, the Islamic study committee issued *fatwas* (religious decrees) and rulings, the media committee published newspapers, the travel committee handled travel documents and tickets, and the finance committee raised money.[11] Outside of its headquarters, first in Sudan and later in Afghanistan, al-Qaeda became very decentralized with regional bureaus linked to cells of 2–15 members each, some with specific specialties, others created for a single operation.[12]

In addition to its central organization and permanent cadre of fighters, al-Qaeda also recruited within target countries. These recruits performed mundane tasks that would have exposed to capture the foreign specialists brought in for an operation. The 1998 bombing of the U.S. embassy in Dar es Salaam, Tanzania, illustrates how al-Qaeda combined such local recruits with professional operatives to carry out a mission. The organization recruited Khalfan Khamis Mohamed in a local mosque, radicalized him, and assigned him to an important jihad mission, but kept him in the dark as to its details. The operational cell had Mohamed rent the safe house the group needed and buy the truck that would carry the explosives. As a local Tanzanian he could perform these duties inconspicuously. The cell brought in an expert to build the bomb, but this specialist and the rest of the cell left the country before Mohamed drove the truck to the embassy on the day of the attack.[13] Many local al-Qaeda members probably never knew the target until the day of the attack. "We, the East Africa cell members, do not want to know about the operations plan since we are just implementers," proclaimed a document found on a computer seized in Tanzania after the attack.[14]

With a presence in 76 countries by 2001, al-Qaeda had become a formidable terrorist organization with global reach.[15] However, the organization's hierarchical structure made it vulnerable. A that time Rohan Gunaratna, one of the world's leading authorities on al-Qaeda, argued that "the most effective state response would be to target al-Qaeda's leadership, cripple its command and control, and disrupt its current and future support bases."[16] Even in late fall 2001, this strategy might have worked, at least against the core organization. However, al-Qaeda has another dimension, a dimension that has grown in importance since 9/11 and which makes it much harder to defeat.

Al-Qaeda the Network

Describing al-Qaeda as a single organization, even one with numerous cells and global reach, does not do it justice. Al-Qaeda also has to be seen as a network, or as a "network of networks," linking numerous organizations hidden within sympathetic populations around the world. While the network aspect of al-Qaeda and its affiliates has evolved and grown in importance since 9/11, it began as the organization itself with the Afghan war against the Soviets.

By drawing in so many mujahedeen from the Muslim world in general and the Arab lands in particular, the conflict created a cadre of dedicated *Jihadists* who could be mobilized by al-Qaeda in the countries to which they returned and/or spawn new terrorist groups of their own. Thousands of men passed through al-Qaeda training camps in Afghanistan, but only a fraction of them stayed with al-Qaeda. Estimates of trainees range from 10,000–110,000 for the period 1989–2001, with no more than 3,000 joining al-Qaeda itself.[17] After the Soviet withdrawal, many mujahedeen went on to fight in Chechnya, Kashmir, and farther abroad. No precise figures on the nationality of these fighters who came to be called the "Afghan Arabs" exist. However, during the early 1990s, the Pakistani government asked Arab militants in their country to register. Though far from complete, the numbers for Northwest Frontier Province, immediately adjacent to Afghanistan, provide a demographic snapshot of the group: "1,142 were Egyptian; 981 Saudis; 946 Sudanese; 792 Algerians; 771 Jordanians; 326 Iraqis; 292 Syrians; 234 Sudanese; 199 Libyans; 117 Tunisians; and 102 Moroccans."[18]

The al-Qaeda network developed further during bin Laden's years in Sudan. In 1995 an Islamic People's Conference met in Khartoum. The conference brought together militants from Algeria, Pakistan, Jordan, Eritrea, Egypt, Yemen, Tunisia, and the Philippines. Al-Qaeda forged links with Hamas, Palestinian Islamic Jihad, and Lebanese Hezbollah, a Shiite group once considered incompatible with the Sunni extremists.[19] In

Febuary 1998 Osama bin Laden announced the formation of a "World Islamic Front for Jihad against Jews and Crusaders." Although known terrorist leaders from groups in Egypt, Pakistan, and Bangladesh signed the agreement forming the alliance, bin Laden kept secret the identities of most organizations gathered under the new umbrella for security reasons.[20]

The importance of al-Qaeda as a network rather than just an organization has increased dramatically since the invasion of Afghanistan. Defeat of the Taliban regime, which had hosted bin Laden and his followers since their expulsion from Sudan, has made it impossible for the terrorist organization to maintain its hierarchical structure. If bin Laden is holed up in the remote southeast border region of Afghanistan and Pakistan, his capacity to control or even influence the course of the terrorist campaign may be considerably reduced. However, the decentralized nature of the terrorist network allows it to be quite effective, albeit in a different way, with little or no direction from the center. Disrupting the command structure in Afghanistan has made it more difficult for al-Qaeda to concentrate and move assets around for an operation like the 1998 embassy bombings. The network has, however, adapted by allowing and/or encouraging affiliates to conduct locally organized, funded, and conducted operations such as the 2004 Madrid and 2005 London bombings.

Al-Qaeda the Movement

Considerable evidence suggests that al-Qaeda may have evolved beyond even the network level. Terrorism analyst Michael Chandler describes what he calls "third generation" terrorism. Bin Laden and his *shura*, the "first generation," directed operations from Afghanistan until the American invasion disrupted their central organization. This invasion sent first-generation al-Qaeda members fleeing to their countries of origin, where they rejoined existing cells and organizations or set up new ones, recruiting the "second generation" of terrorists. In addition to these affiliates, the last few years have seen the rise of new, "third generation" groups whose members have no experience of Afghanistan or even a direct connection to those who trained there. The al-Qaeda parent organization provides inspiration, guidance, and perhaps some material support rather than exercising direct control. Third-generation terrorists constitute themselves, raise funds, plan, and even conduct operations, and then seek al-Qaeda's blessing.[21]

The London bombings of July 7 and 21, 2005 provide an example of this latest manifestation of al-Qaeda terror. The four suicide bombers met at a

Muslim Community Center attached to a Mosque in Leeds, England. Three were under the age of 24, and only one had been born outside the United Kingdom, a nineteen-year old youth from Jamaica. None had a criminal record. Only one member of the group seems to have had a clear connection to anyone outside the community. Mohammad Sidique Khan had traveled to Pakistan, where he presumably received training in bomb making. He probably recruited the other three members to form a "self-contained cell" that manufactured the bombs locally and may even have chosen the targets. The attack has been described by British officials as "a transformation in extremism in recent years: Operatives with British roots replaced foreigners, predominantly North Africans and Gulf Arabs as the primary threat here."[22] Lack of direction from more experienced al-Qaeda leaders may explain some of the more amateur aspects of the attack, such as failing to detonate all the bombs in deep tube lines where they would have been more lethal (26 of the dead were on the only targeted train in a deep tunnel) and leaving a car with explosives and other evidence at a car park in Luton the day of the attack.

Two weeks later a second, less successful attack occurred against the London commuter system. This attack failed miserably because the detonators on the backpack bombs failed to ignite the main charges. British security forces rapidly apprehended the perpetrators and gleaned a mass of intelligence information that remains classified. Italian police arrested another terrorist trying to flee Europe via Rome. That terrorist claimed that his groups launched the second attack to honor the martyrs of July 7, but the authorities have not ruled out a connection between the two operations.[23] Similarities between the London attacks and the Madrid bombings of the previous year suggest that July 21 may have been the second phase of a complex operation.

This new phase in the evolution of al-Qaeda has been made possible by the Internet. Cyberspace has become the new staging area for attacks. Terrorists use the Internet to spread their message, raise money, recruit members and even direct operations. In the words of General John Abizaid, Commander, U.S. Central Command, "The only safe haven that remains for al-Qaeda is the virtual realm."[24] The general may underestimate the number of physical havens within sympathetic populations in real space, but he rightly warns about the cyber threat. Former head of the CIA's bin Laden unit, Mike Sheuer, shares this concern about the worldwide web: "The current state of al-Qaeda and the health of al-Qaeda is largely due to its ability to manipulate the Internet."[25] According to terrorism expert Peter Bergen, one of the few Westerners to interview the al-Qaeda leader, "Bin Laden and his followers have exploited twenty-first-century communications and weapons technology in the service of the most extreme, retrograde reading of holy war. The result is a fusion I call Holy War, Inc."[26]

Terrorist Profiles

Conventional wisdom has that 9/11 tore up the guide book on who becomes a terrorist. Mohammed Atta and his associates did not come from the ranks of the downtrodden on the dirt tracks of refugee camps. They came from comfortable middle class homes, earned college degrees, and had lived abroad. The London bombers also did not fit the traditional terrorist profile. Osama bin Laden was a millionaire and his inner circle came from the ranks of the prosperous and educated.

This apparent change in terrorist recruiting patterns should not, however, be overemphasized. Poor youths still make up the bulk of suicide bombers sent through Syria to die in Iraq. Despite their relative prosperity, the London bombers were still impressionable young men as was the front man recruited for the Dar es Salaam bombing. The London youths came from England's northern rust built city of Leeds, where minority communities remain ghettoized and face blatant discrimination and intermittent attack. Even the well-off and educated can experience the "hopelessness and helplessness" that impel people to violence. Bin Laden and his lieutenants confirm rather than deviate from the traditional profile. Insurgent and terrorist group leaders have seldom come from the lower classes, whose energy must be spent in staying alive rather than planning revolution. Lenin's father was a minor noble, Mao Tse-Tung and Ho Chi Minh both came from prosperous backgrounds, and most RAF members came from the West German middle class.

Once again, al-Qaeda terrorism has not so much defied historic patterns as broadened them. The poor, marginalized, and disenfranchised still provide a deep pool of recruits. These recruits will now be joined, however, by the disillusioned children of immigrants in Europe and America. Young men in their early teens and twenties will still form the core of suicide bombers, but they will be joined by men and even women in their late twenties and thirties, people with families and, one would think, much reason to live.

Operations

Although bin Laden decided to target the United States during or immediately after the 1991 Gulf War, Americans remained largely unaware of al-Qaeda's existence. The United States thus misinterpreted a series of related attacks as separate incidents rather than operations belonging to a single strategic campaign. If anyone in the intelligence community saw a larger pattern, they did not have the ear of decision makers. Failure to understand the new threat and respond to it effectively certainly emboldened the terrorists and increased the vulnerability of the American homeland.

In 1993, the radical Egyptian cleric Sheik Omar Abdul Rahman (also known as the Blind Sheik) masterminded an attack upon the World Trade Center. In cooperation with Ramsi Ahmed Yousef, the Sheik led a group calling itself the Liberation Army Fifth Battalion to plant a truck bomb made from fertilizer laced with accelerant underneath the building. Six people died in the attack, which caused $4.5 million dollars in damage but did no lasting harm to the structure. The terrorists opposed U.S. support for Israel and interference in the Middle East.[27] In retrospect the group's rhetoric indicated its al-Qaeda sympathies if not direct affiliation, but in 1993 few if any in the West knew that bin Laden's organization even existed. Al-Qaeda did, however, fund the attack.[28]

That same year U.S. forces in Somalia as part of a UN mission to safeguard humanitarian relief and promote stability in the war torn country suffered a devastating attack. On October 3, 1993, Army Rangers and Delta Force Commandos deployed in Mogadishu to capture warlord Mohammed Farah Aidid faced determined resistance from the General's forces as they withdrew from his headquarters. The Somalis shot down a Blackhawk helicopter and ambushed a rescue party sent to retrieve the crew. Aidid's militiamen dragged some of the bodies through the streets in front of television cameras. The humiliating incident led directly to American withdrawal. Once again, the intelligence community seems to have missed the larger context in which the attack took place. In a 1997 interview bin Laden acknowledged al-Qaeda's role in the affair. "With Allah's grace," the terrorist leader proclaimed, "Muslims in Somalia cooperated with some Arab holy warriors who were in Afghanistan. Together they killed large numbers of American occupation troops." The Afghan Arabs may have applied the skills they developed in attacking Soviet helicopters to shoot down the Blackhawk.[29]

Two years later the terrorists struck again, this time against a target in bin Laden's homeland. On November 13, 1995, a joint al-Qaeda-Hezbollah operation detonated a van packed with Semtex outside the Khobar Towers, a U.S. military complex in Riyadh, Saudi Arabia. The blast killed six people and injured sixty. Several Islamic groups (other than the real perpetrators) claimed responsibility for the attack.[30] No one in the intelligence community seems to have seen a connection with the World Trade Center bombing or with a thwarted plan to blow up airliners from the Manila airport over the Pacific the previous year (another of the blind Sheik's schemes). Few at the time could have imagined the radical Sunni organization al-Qaeda cooperating with the equally militant Shiite group Hezbollah.

It would take another three years and a devastating attack against American embassies in East Africa before the Unites States would begin to connect the dots. In what has become al-Qaeda's signature method, terrorists launched near simultaneous attacks on the U.S. embassies in

Nairobi, Kenya and Dar es Salaam, Tanzania on August 7, 1998. The Nairobi bombing killed 291 people, most of them Kenyans, and injured 5,000. The Dar es Salaam attack killed 10 and injured 77.[31] The capture of one of the Tanzanian terrorists made it possible to pin the attack firmly on bin Laden, who eventually accepted responsibility for the attack.

Following the embassy bombings the United States took military action, launching cruise missiles at al-Qaeda training camps in Afghanistan and destroying a pharmaceutical factory in Sudan. The camp attacks proved wholly ineffective and may have encouraged bin Laden to believe that he could not be reached in his mountain sanctuary. No definitive evidence that the Sudanese factory had ever been used to produce chemical weapons as the Clinton administration claimed has ever been produced, so that operation proved to be a public relations nightmare. The administration did, however, achieve some success in foiling terrorist plots designed to coincide with millennium celebrations on New Years Eve 1999/2000, particularly a plan to bomb Los Angeles's LAX airport.

Success, however, proved short-lived. On October 12, 2000, the American warship U.S.S. Cole lay at anchor in Aden harbor, Yemen, where it had stopped to refuel. Suicide bombers piloted a small boat loaded with explosives up to the ship and detonated it. The explosion killed 17, wounded 39, and very nearly sank the vessel. The Cole, like the Khobar Towers, was a military target, so a purist might argue that the attack should not be classified as terrorism. The incident did, however, add one more piece to an emerging intelligence puzzle that clearly revealed a strategic, low-level campaign against the United States. Despite new awareness of al-Qaeda and growing appreciation of the group's extent and complexity, the American public and perhaps the U.S. government remained blissfully naïve about homeland security. With the exception of the largely ineffectual 1993 World Trade Center bombing, which had yet to be definitively linked to al-Qaeda, attacks by Islamic extremists had been against American interests overseas. Few people imagined that the a catastrophic attack could occur at home, a confidence reflected in the absurd practice of applying intense security measures for international flights but significantly relaxed ones for domestic.

The price for failing to see the pattern in a decade of coordinated al-Qaeda operations was, of course, 9/11. Plans for the attack had been in motion for 3–5 years, and at least some of the terrorists entered the country a year before conducting their mission. As the *9/11 Report* amply demonstrates, the attacks caught everyone from the President down to the lowest paid screener at Boston's Logan Airport completely by surprise. Two airliners struck the twin towers of the World Trade Center, and a third hit the Pentagon. Were it not for the courage of its forty-four passengers, who forced the hijackers to down the plane in a Pennsylvania field, a fourth airliner would have found its target, possibly the White House or the Capitol Building. Another 2,749 people died in the Towers and 189 at the Pentagon. The attacks injured almost 2,500 others.[32] The economic impact in direct and indirect costs has yet to be calculated, but certainly amounts to billions of dollars.

Since 9/11 al-Qaeda's ability to mount a large scale attack against the United States has probably been hampered by the disruption of its safe haven in Afghanistan. It has, however, conducted successful operations in Turkey, Indonesia, Afghanistan, Pakistan, Spain, and the United Kingdom. On March 11, 2004, terrorists detonated a series of bombs on commuter trains and in a station in Madrid, Spain, killing 191 people. A little known al-Qaeda affiliate claimed credit for the attack, although the explosives used were similar to those employed by ETA, fueling fear that Basque terrorists had perhaps formed an unholy alliance with the Islamic extremists. The incident led to the defeat of Prime Minister Jose Azner's party in national elections a few days later. Far from "knuckling under" to terrorism, Spanish voters were angered by Azner's rush to blame ETA for the Madrid bombings and by his earlier willingness to send troops to Iraq contrary to the wishes of the vast majority of Spaniards. Many observers, however, saw the new government's decision to withdraw its contingent from the American-led coalition and the terrorists' subsequent promise not to attack Spain again as an al-Qaeda victory.

The Madrid Bombings encouraged the European Union (EU) to take the terrorist threat more seriously. The EU Council issued a Declaration on Combating Terrorism and specifically tasked a unit within the EU Commission with the "Fight against terrorism, trafficking and exploitation of human beings and law enforcement co-operation." As might be expected agreement on defensive measures such as protecting ports and infrastructure has been easier to achieve than consensus on how to attack terrorist organizations. These bureaucratic measures have, however, not produced adequate security. European infrastructure, public buildings and other potential targets generally remain more vulnerable than their American counterparts.

Just over a year following the Madrid attacks, four suicide bombers attacked the London underground, detonating almost simultaneously three bombs on trains during rush hour on July 7, 2005. A fourth bomber blew himself up on a double-decker bus about an hour later. The attack killed 52 people, including the four suicide bombers, and injured several hundred others. Three of the four bombers had been born in the United Kingdom, and all four were relatively well educated and middle class. Two apparently had wives (one of whom was pregnant) and children. Family, friends, and neighbors described the men as religious but in no way suspected them of a connection to any terrorist organization.[33] The group calling itself the Abu Hafs Al-Masri Brigade left behind a video in which its leader claimed responsibility for the bombings. "Until we feel security, you will be our targets," the group's oldest member and apparent leader Mohammed Sidique Khan (age 30) proclaimed. "Until you stop the bombing, gassing, imprisonment and torture of my people, we will not stop this fight."[34]

The al-Qaeda Organization in the Land of the Two Rivers (more commonly known as "al-Qaeda in Iraq"), a terrorist organization led by Abu Musab al-Zarqawi (until his death in June 2006) and affiliated with al-Qaeda proper, has mounted weekly attacks against U.S. forces since the 2003 invasion of Iraq. The group also targets members of the emerging Iraqi security forces, government officials, and ordinary civilians deemed supportive of or just too friendly with the Americans. In November 2005, the group simultaneously bombed three hotels in Amman, Jordan, killing over 60 people and injuring more than 100 others in an effort to stop Jordan from supporting the U.S.-led war in Iraq.[35]

In addition to these actual attacks dozens of other plots around the world have probably been foiled, although such information would not be made public. Although the United States has not suffered a direct attack since 9/11, the government must take seriously the possibility that other operations against the American homeland are underway. It did, after all, take 3–5 years to plan the 9/11 attacks, so it is impossible to say for certain that similar plots have not already been launched.

Conclusion

Al-Qaeda is not a completely new phenomenon. It represents the latest manifestation of the historical evolution of terrorism over the past century and a half enhanced by broader social, political, economic, and technological developments. The terrorists have gone global for the same reason that multinational corporations, criminals, and other organizations have gone global: a revolution in telecommunications and the Internet in particular makes it possible for them to do so.

Al-Qaeda is complex but not unfathomable and certainly not unbeatable. Understanding it on several levels is the key to defeating it. Al-Qaeda is an organization, a network of organizations and an extremist movement that inspires would-be followers to join it or to emulate its activities. The threat it poses must be combated on each of these levels. However, devising a successful counterterrorism strategy requires understanding not only al-Qaeda but its motives.

CHAPTER 5

What Do the Terrorists Want?

Prevailing Myths

In the years since 9/11 Americans have persistently asked two troubling questions: Why does al-Qaeda hate us, and what specifically does the group want? Neither question can be easily answered, and both have elicited glib, simplistic, and very unhelpful responses. The assumption that the terrorists and their supporters hate the American way of life has obscured its very specific and regionally focused political objectives. Al-Qaeda's religious ideology has led to dangerous misperceptions of a monolithic Islam inimical to Western values and encouraged Americans to treat all Muslims as suspect, including nearly six million of their fellow citizens. Perhaps equally problematic is an academic tendency to dismiss the broad Islamist movement of which al-Qaeda terrorism is the most extreme example as a mere aberration within the larger faith.

Like everything else about al-Qaeda, its concrete objectives and broader ideological goals are complex. Fortunately, the organization and its supporters have stated their beliefs and demands numerous times over the past decade. Many of these demands are quite understandable and cannot be easily dismissed as the irrational ravings of religious fanatics. Broad segments of the Muslim world accept at least some of al-Qaeda's goals even if the overwhelming majority disapproves of its terrorist methods. The larger religious movement from which al-Qaeda draws inspiration must also be seriously examined rather than glibly dismissed as bad theology. Only by understanding both its immediate goals and its long-term objectives can al-Qaeda and its affiliates be effectively combated.

Restoring Islamic Rule

The series of attacks culminating in 9/11 obscure the important fact that al-Qaeda has never considered the United States its primary target. Osama bin Laden and his associates set as their ultimate goal reestablishment of the *uma* or community of Muslims in a caliphate. This religious mission invokes a vision of early Islam during which Muslims lived in a theocratic state governed first by the Prophet Mohammed and then by his successors the Caliphs. However utopian this goal may seem, it leads to a very specific and immediate objective: removal of secular and heretical governments in the Muslim world. Egypt, birthplace of pan-Arab secular nationalism, offers the best example of the first, and Saudi Arabia, a theocratic state whose rulers have deviated (according to bin Laden) from the true teachings of Islam, represents the second.

Long before the creation of al-Qaeda, Islamic extremists opposed the government of Egypt. In response to the post-colonial secular nationalism of Egypt's first President Gamal Abdel Nasser, the religious scholar Sayd Qutb proposed a return to the true religion of the Prophet. For Qutb nationalism and socialism were the great idols of the day. This stance and his membership in the Muslim Brotherhood, an Islamic organization banned by Nasser in 1954, landed Qutb in prison and led to his execution in 1966.[1] Qutb's writing profoundly influenced Osama bin Laden, who had been mentored by Qutb's brother while at university. During the heady days of pan-Arab pride following Nasser's seizure of the Suez Canal from Britain, "Islamism," as the teaching of Qutb and those who share his views is called, seemed doomed to fade away, an outdated concept better suited to an earlier time. Humiliating defeat at the hands of the Israelis during the Six-Day War of 1967, and the declining economic strength of the country encouraged belief that the future of Egypt and indeed of all Muslim countries lay not in the direction of Western secular democracy but in a return to the nation's Islamic roots. The Muslim Brotherhood's slogan, "The Koran is our constitution," epitomized this view.[2]

Egyptian Islamism radicalized and became more violent as Islamic Jihad emerged in the 1970s as the successor to the more moderate Muslim Brotherhood. The group sought violent overthrow of the regime, and in 1981 it assassinated Nasser's successor Anwar Sadat. Besides being a secular ruler, Sadat had committed the unforgivable sin of making peace with Israel by signing the Camp David Accords (1978). Egyptian Islamic Jihad (to distinguish it from other terrorist groups who use the same name) sent many *mujahedeen* to Afghanistan to fight the Soviets. Osama bin Laden's second in command Ayman al-Zawahiri formerly headed the organization. Al-Zawahiri devotes much of his memoir, *Knights under the Prophet's Banner*, to the Egyptian struggle. He pays tribute to Qutb and preaches the ideology that motivates both Islamic Jihad and al-Qaeda:

> Sayyid Qutb's call for loyalty to God's oneness and to acknowledge God's sole authority and sovereignty was the spark that ignited the Islamic revolution against the enemies of Islam at home and abroad. The bloody chapters of this revolution continue to unfold day after day.[3]

Egypt leads the list of Muslim states with secular governments al-Qaeda wants to replace with religious ones. Turkey, Algeria, and Pakistan fall into the same category. In each of these countries the army has been the bulwark of the secular order. Turkey's military has intervened more than once to preserve Mustapha Kemal (Ataturk)'s modernist revolution, and the Algerian army set aside a 1991 election that put the Islamic Salvation Front, the country's Islamist party, in power. In Pakistan General Pervez Musharif, who seized power in a 1999 coup and declared himself president in 2001, maintains a tenuous hold with U.S. support over a country in which many people would prefer a more religious state.

Ironically, Saddam Hussein also figured prominently on al-Qaeda's list of leaders who needed to be removed from power. The Iraqi dictator led one of the most brutal regimes in the Middle East, and failed either to live or to govern as a devout Muslim. His scandalous moral behavior and especially that of his two sons added to his list of sins. On the eve of the 2003 invasion bin Laden expressed sympathy and support for the Iraqi people, not their leader. Whatever else the United States achieved by removing the dictator, it unwittingly accomplished one of al-Qaeda's goals.

While bin Laden objects to governments like that of Egypt for their secularism, he opposes the Saudi regime for its apostasy. Bin Laden did not, however, initially target the land of his birth. The kingdom, governed by Islamic sharia law since its creation, seemed to be the kind of state the al-Qaeda leader envisioned. However, the monarchy's decision to invite American troops into the country during the 1991 Gulf War persuaded him that the regime had become a tool of the United States and was beyond hope of redemption. In any event, the uma envisioned by the Islamists was to be governed by a limited form of republic based on a principle of limited consultation known as *shura*, not monarchy. Since 1991, bin Laden has repeatedly castigated the Saudi regime. "By being loyal to the U.S. regime," he told Peter Arnett in a March 1997 CNN interview, "the Saudi government has committed an act against Islam. And this, based on the ruling of Shari'a (Islamic jurisprudence), casts the regime outside the religious community."[4] Being "outside the religious community" means the monarchy can be legitimately removed by force if necessary. Bin Laden gave the Saudi regime two choices: "bring back Islamic law, and . . . practice real Shura (consultative government)" or be overthrown. [5]

Fighting the Great Satan

With bin Laden and his followers focused so resolutely on the Muslim world, how did the United States become a target? American intervention in the Persian Gulf to drive Saddam Hussein out of Kuwait and remove the threat to Saudi Arabia confirmed a growing al-Qaeda belief that it could accomplish none of its goals in the Muslim world as long as the world's last superpower meddled in Islamic affairs. Egyptian President Hosni Mubarak, who succeeded Sadat in 1981 and has remained in power ever since, has been propped up by massive U.S. foreign aide as part of the Camp David Accords. The United States not only defiled the sacred soil of Saudi Arabia during the Gulf War but failed to leave once it had ended. The American military maintained forces in the kingdom and established bases in other Gulf States. This continued American presence led bin Laden and others to assume that the United States aimed to permanently dominate the region. He praised the attack on the Khobar Towers (though he did not take credit for it), saying of the victims, "these are the troops who left their country and their families and came here with all arrogance to steal our oil and disgrace us, and attack our religion."[6]

Bin Laden's rhetoric against the United States heated up with the increasing intensity of his attacks. "We declared jihad [in this context, "Holy War"] against the US government, because the US government is unjust, criminal and tyrannical," he proclaimed in the 1997 CNN interview. "It has committed acts that are extremely unjust, hideous and criminal whether directly or through its support of the Israeli occupation of the Prophet's Night Travel Land (Palestine)." He went on to blame the U.S. government for the death of 6,000 Iraqi children because of the embargo that denied them food and medical supplies. First and foremost, however, he wanted U.S. military forces and civilian personnel out of Saudi Arabia. Significantly, bin Laden distinguished between the government and the American people. "We have focused our declaration on striking at the soldiers in the country of the Two Holy Places [Mecca and Medina]," he explained but went on to say that since he could not guarantee the safety of civilians, they would have to leave Saudi Arabia as well. Asked if an American withdrawal from the country would bring an end to jihad, bin Laden warned that "jihad against the US does not stop with its withdrawal from the Arabian Peninsula, but rather it must desist from aggressive intervention against Muslims in the whole world."[7] In a different interview he explained that "in our religion it is our duty to make jihad so that God's word is the one exalted to the heights and so that we drive the Americans away from all Muslim countries."[8]

Al-Qaeda's distinction between civilian and military would soon disappear, if bin Laden ever really made it in the first place. In his infamous *fatwa* (religious proclamation) of February 23, 1998, issued on behalf of the "World Islamic Front," bin Laden declared war on the American people. His proclamation asserted the usual grievances: occupation of the Arabian Peninsula and suffering inflicted on the Iraqi people by military action and sanctions. "All these crimes and sins committed by the Americans are a clear declaration of war on Allah, his messenger, and

Muslims," the decree proclaimed. In keeping with traditional Islamic teaching, bin Laden called for a defensive war to protect Islam and the Muslim uma. "In compliance with Allah's order," he issued his fatwa to all Muslims:

> The ruling to kill the Americans and their allies—civilians and military—is an individual duty for every Muslim who can do it in any country in which it is possible to do it, in order to liberate the al-Aqsa Mosque [Jerusalem] and the holy mosque [Mecca] from their grip, and in order for their armies to move out of all the lands of Islam, defeated and unable to threaten any Muslim. This is in accordance with the words of Almighty Allah, "and fight the pagans all together as they fight you all together," and "fight them until there is no more tumult or oppression, and there prevail justice and faith in Allah."[9]

Although bin Laden laced the fatwa with verses from the *Holy Quran*, he ignored the Prophet's admonition to spare noncombatants in general and women and children in particular.

Surprisingly, the fatwa does not single out Israel as a focus of al-Qaeda outrage. Bin Laden only mentions the state indirectly, calling for the liberation of Jerusalem's al Aqsa Mosque. Although an important concern, the Israeli-Palestinian conflict has never been the core issue in al-Qaeda's ideology. Without the Gulf War and the "occupation" of Saudi Arabia, U.S. support for Israel would probably not by itself have led to the current terrorist campaign. However, the conflict has figured more prominently in recent al-Qaeda propaganda, perhaps because it resonates with so much of the Arab world. In an October 30, 2004, speech broadcast on Aljazeera television, bin Laden referred to the "American/Israeli coalition against our people in Palestine and Lebanon."[10]

Al-Qaeda has also embraced the Nazi belief in Jewish conspiracies. The fatwa calling for attacks on Americans does so as part of a jihad against "Crusaders and Jews." "Crusader" refers to the medieval Christian invaders of the Holy Land but has become a synonym for Americans, reflecting al-Qaeda's religious worldview. Bin Laden and his supporters see the United States, Israel, and the Jews as inextricably linked. In his numerous interviews, speeches, and fatwas he alternately describes Israel as America's client state in the Middle East and asserts that the American government does the bidding of the Jews.

Since 9/11 bin Laden and his associates have continued to insist that they are fighting a defensive war against U.S. led aggression. The 2003 invasion of Iraq made these claims much easier to sell to the larger Arab and Muslim worlds. As occurred in Afghanistan following the Soviet invasion, mujahedeen have poured into the country to cooperate with indigenous forces to fight the invader. Getting the United States out of

Muslim countries as a prelude to Islamic revolution within them remains the primary goal of the movement. A letter purported to be from al-Qaeda second-in-command al-Zawahiri to al-Qaeda in Iraq leader Abu Musab al-Zarqawi delineates a four-stage strategy for achieving this goal:

1. expel the Americans from Iraq;
2. establish an Iraqi Islamic emirate as a prelude to joining the wider caliphate;
3. extend the jihad to secular states surrounding Iraq;
4. clash with Israel, which was established to challenge any new Islamic entity.[11]

Combating Secularism

In addition to expelling Americans from the Muslim world, al-Qaeda would also like to stop the equally pernicious erosion of Islamic values by a decadent Western culture. The Internet, satellite television, and the broader phenomenon to which they belong have barraged Muslims (and everyone else) with a plethora of objectionable messages and even more offensive images. Unlike books and magazines, the new electronic delivery systems cannot be easily censored. Their content seems to promote materialism, promiscuity, and secularism. In the words of one scholar of globalization, "'immorality' is just a click away," and "satellite transmissions need no visa."[12] Bin Laden warned that the new media served "to drowse the community, and to fulfill the plans of the enemies through keeping the people occupied with minor matters, and to stir their emotions and desires until corruption becomes widespread amongst the believers."[13] In a recruiting tape widely circulated during the summer of 2001, he complained that when U.S. troops deployed to Saudi Arabia, "these Americans brought . . . Jewish women who can go anywhere in our holy land."[14] The sight of Western women free to drive, associate with men, and go about with their hair uncovered offended both al-Qaeda and many Saudis who do not support terrorism. Bin Laden's ally al-Zarqawi described the war in Iraq in similar terms as a clash between Western values and the true religion of Islam:

> The enemies of God are aware that this war is a turning point in the world, that it is a choice between an absolute control of the infidel West, its culture, and way of life and the Islamic renaissance which is coming, God willing.[15]

Six years prior to 9/11 and before most Americans had even heard of al-Qaeda, political scientist Benjamin R. Barber warned of a growing conflict between "Jihad" and "McWorld." Barber argued that globalization was actually stimulating violent backlashes in areas of the world suddenly open to the corrupting influence. For Barber, "jihad" served only as a metaphor for resistance to globalization, although he did acknowledge that such resistance would be most intense in the Muslim world. "McWorld is a product of popular culture driven by expansionist commerce," Barber declared.[16] Fear for the loss of national, religious, and/or cultural identity fueled the resistance. McWorld and Jihad are, however, also codependent. McWorld depends on global markets and must adapt its marketing strategies to local custom. Jihad opposes McWorld by appropriating its tools, particularly the Internet and television, to build a worldwide base of support for resistance.[17]

Although Barber considers *jihad* as both antidemocratic and antimodern, the reality of the al-Qaeda struggle is much more complex. Rather than opposing "modernity," the terrorists and, more importantly, the broader population that support their goals if not their methods offer a vision of the future different from the free-market, secular world the current U.S. administration seeks to create. Rather than oppose democracy, they resist the neo-conservative, free-market, secular version of it foisted upon the Muslim World by the United States and its allies.[18]

A Matter of Priorities

If al-Qaeda has both specific regional political goals and the broader objective of resisting the incursion of Western culture, which aim predominates? Should the United States withdraw from the Islamic world in general, would the terrorist attacks stop, or would the terrorists simply broaden their list of targets in what would become Huntington's clash of civilizations? Although these questions cannot be answered with certainty, al-Qaeda's target list to date suggests its priorities. When the organization aims directly at the United States it chooses without fail military, political, and economic targets: U.S. forces in Somalia and Saudi Arabia, the U.S.S. Cole in Aden, the American Embassies in East Africa, and on 9/11, the Twin Towers and the Pentagon, symbols, respectively, of American economic and military power.

Within majority Muslim countries, however, attacks sometimes follow a different pattern. The burning of a Kentucky Fried Chicken restaurant in Pakistan following 9/11 may have been amusing, but it is also very revealing. The fast-food franchise represents the intrusion of Western culture, materialism, and secular values. The deadly Bali bombing of October 12, 2002, targeted a resort area frequented by Australian and other western tourists, who may have been the primary targets. The attack killed 202 and injured 300. However, when al-Qaeda claimed responsibility for the attack, it noted that it had targeted "nightclubs and whorehouses in Indonesia."[19] A series of three bomb attacks against tourists at the Egyptian resort of Sharm El-Sheikh on July 23, 2005 killed eighty people in what Egyptian authorities claimed was a locally motivated incident.[20] Once again, the terrorists targeted resort hotels with their casinos, more manifestations of Western decadence.

Al-Qaeda's target selection strongly suggests that the terrorists' primary goal is getting the United States and its allies out of Muslim countries. It consistently targets symbols or manifestations of economic, military, and political power. Attacks on manifestations of Western decadence and cultural intrusion usually occur when these targets appear within Muslim states. The message seems clear: leave our countries and let us decide what activities are and are not appropriate for our people.

Islam, Islamism, and the Use of Terror

Since religious ideology drives al-Qaeda extremism, that ideology must be appropriately situated within the larger religion to which it belongs. In trying to understand the relationship between terrorism motivated by Islam and Islam itself, Western analysts frequently make two broad errors. They either see Islam as an irrational religion with a strong tendency to violence, or they dismiss Islamic extremism as a mere perversion of the religion by a handful of radicals. Neither assessment does justice to the complexity of the situation. To understand al-Qaeda one must understand both Islam and *Islamism*, a broad reform movement from which the terrorist organization derives many of its beliefs.

As the third of the Abrahamic faiths, Islam has much in common with both Judaism and Christianity. All three religions are monotheistic, although Islam rejects the Christian trinity as does Judaism. Contrary to a popular belief held by some conservative Christians, "Allah" is not a pagan deity but merely the Arabic word for "God," akin to the Hebrew "Elohim." "Islam" literally means "submission to the will of Allah," and a "Muslim" is "one who submits." Islam, like Christianity and unlike Judaism, seeks converts. Indeed, proclaiming *Tawhid* ("the oneness of God") is the first duty of every Muslim. Despite its commitment to proselytizing, Islam has historically been far more tolerant of Jews and Christians than Christianity has been of Muslims or Jews. The *Holy Quran*, the sacred scriptures revealed to the Prophet Mohammed beginning in 610 CE, identifies Christians and Jews as "people of the book," children of God who received earlier revelations through God's other prophets (Abraham, Moses, Jesus). Muslims should try to convert (or "reconvert" since everyone is born in submission to Allah) Jews and Christians, whose scriptures have been corrupted, but it must never persecute them or force them to accept Islam. Muslims did not always uphold this doctrine of tolerance, but Islamic civilization did not produce anything like the European pogroms or the Roman Catholic Inquisition. In fact, Jews fled Catholic Spain for the more tolerant realms of the Ottoman Turkish Empire following the fall of the Moorish Kingdom of Granada in 1492.

Soon after Mohammed's death a dispute arose that would eventually divide the Muslim world into its two main branches, Sunni and Shiite Islam. Like all rulers of the ancient world Mohammed had both religious and political authority, which could not have been separated. Upon Mohammed's death his followers argued over who should succeed him. The majority believed that the keeper of the Prophet's *sunnah* (traditions) should be chosen from among his followers by the principal of *shura* (consultation). This group became known as "Sunnis." Mohammed's cousin and son-in-law Ali maintained that the *Caliph* should be a member of the Prophet's own family and claimed the title for himself and his line as the father of the Prophet's only direct descendents. Those who supported this interpretation of Mohammed's wishes called themselves "partisans of Ali," "*Shiite*" in Arabic. Ali became the fourth Caliph in 658 but ruled only until 661 when a rebel soldier assassinated him. Sunnis regained and maintained control of the Caliphate which passed from Arab to Ottoman Turkish control in the middle ages and disappeared in 1924 when Mustapha Kemal established the modern secular state of Turkey. Most Shiites have historically followed the teachings of 12 Imams beginning with Ali himself and ending with Muhammad Ali Mahdi, who was born in 868 and in 874 disappeared from human view. Ali Mahdi will remain hidden until he returns to complete his work of making Islam the global religion.[21]

Other doctrinal differences divide Sunni and Shiite Islam, but two in particular relate to discussion of insurgency and terrorism, albeit indirectly. Because Shiites grant religious scholars considerable authority to interpret the Holy Quran, their clergy play a greater role in religious life and politics than do Sunni Imams. This difference explains why clerics like Grand Ayatollah Sayyid Ali Husaini Sistani enjoy such power and influence in contemporary Iraq. Osama bin Laden and his followers generally consider Shiites "*Kafirs*" (non-believers), which makes his alliance with Hezbollah rather remarkable. Concentrated in Iran, Iraq, Lebanon, and Bahrain, Shiites make up 11% of all Muslims.[22]

Like all the great world religions, Islam has spawned its share of violence. The Prophet had to fight a long conflict with the rulers of Mecca so that the new religion would survive. This conflict gave rise to the concept of *jihad*, derived from the verb *jhd*, meaning "to strive or exert oneself." Following defeat of the forces of Mecca in the Battle of the Trenches before Medina, the Prophet explained that warfare in defense of Islam, which had just occurred, is the "lesser jihad." The "greater jihad" is the struggle each Muslim undertakes throughout his/her life to submit to the will of Allah, to live a righteous life, to be a good Muslim.[23] According to the Prophet, lesser jihad must be conducted according to guidelines that meet the standards of Christian "just war theory." In particular, Muslim soldiers must distinguish between combatants and noncombatants and make every effort to spare women and children.

Given that al-Qaeda and it affiliates call themselves "Jihadists," do their actions fit the exacting standards of defensive warfare according to the humanitarian guidelines set down by the Prophet? The immediate response would be, "of course not!" al-Qaeda kills men, women, and children, combatants and noncombatants indiscriminately. According to *Al-Hayat*, Islamic Research Council of al-Azhar University,

> Islam provides clear rules and ethical norms that forbid the killing of non-combatants, as well as women, children, and the elderly, and also forbids the pursuit of the enemy in defeat, the execution of those who surrender, the infliction of harm on prisoners of war, and the destruction of property that is not being used in the hostilities.[24]

Al-Qaeda clearly seems to act outside these guidelines.

Once again, however, the reality of the situation may not be so straightforward. Bin Laden has always maintained that al-Qaeda fights a defensive war against an aggressive United States that increasingly interferes in the affairs of Muslim states. Neither the organization nor its affiliates attacked American targets until after U.S. forces entered Saudi Arabia. Until 9/11 al-Qaeda generally avoided killing civilians. The October 3 incident in Somalia (1993), the bombing of the Khobar Towers in Riyadh (1995), and the attack on the U.S.S. Cole (2000) aimed at military targets within Muslim countries. Without justifying these attacks, one can question whether they should really be called terrorism and at least recognize that many people in the Muslim world might deem such actions legitimate. Many civilians died in the East African embassy bombings (1998), few of them Americans, but bin Laden justified even this attack by saying that the American Embassy in East Africa housed a major intelligence collection center. Virtually all American embassies do have at the very least a CIA station chief.

The 9/11 attacks did not, of course, conform to any just-war criteria. With the exception of those who died in the Pentagon, none of the casualties had anything to do with U.S. policy. Even if al-Qaeda and its supporters believed their own absurd rhetoric that those who worked in the Twin Towers controlled the levers of global economic imperialism, nothing could justify the deaths of innocent civilians on four aircraft, at least one of which contained school children on a field trip.

Israel's illegal occupation of the West Bank and Gaza and the American occupation of Iraq further justify al-Qaeda's claim to be waging a legitimate jihad in defense of Islam, at least in the eyes of its supporters and perhaps many moderate Muslims as well. Again without condoning such acts, the United States must realize that attacks upon its service personnel and the emerging Iraqi security forces can be justified as legitimate resistance by those who perpetrate them. Similarly, Hamas, the al-Aqsa Martyrs' Brigades, and Palestinian Islamic Jihad see themselves as waging a legitimate defensive war against an illegal occupation. Significantly, none of these organizations has carried out missions against non-Israeli targets abroad or attacked the many Christian tourists who visit the country each year.[25] This observation does not excuse suicide bombing of Israelis or anyone else, but it does clarify the context in which terrorist attacks occur.

Comforting as it might be to dismiss bin Laden's theology as a mere aberration within Islam, doing so distorts reality, at least to some degree. Al-Qaeda represents the most extreme manifestation of a reform movement within contemporary Islam. "Islamism" refers to a broad ideological effort to apply the teachings of Islam to the challenges of the contemporary world, particularly those presented by the spread of the Western ideologies of capitalism, communism, and socialism in the Muslim world.[26]

Islamism has its roots in but differs considerably from an early Islamic revival movement known as *Salafism.*. The *Salafist* movement originated in the ninth century but was more fully expounded by the fourteenth-century Islamic scholar, Taqi al-Din Ahmad Ibn Taymiyya. Salafism, from the Arabic word *salaf* meaning devout ancestor (in reference to the first generation of Muslims) calls for a return to the true teachings of the first uma, the community to which the Prophet Mohammed himself belonged. Ibn Taymiyya deviated from the orthodox Sunni Muslim teaching forbidding rebellion against Muslim rulers, and allowed jihad against heretical leaders.[27] The nineteenth century saw a revival of Salafism in Egypt, Persia (Iran), and Syria, perhaps as a response to imperialism and colonialism.[28]

During the eighteenth century a variant of Salafism arose in the Arabian Peninsula. Muhammad Ibn Abd al-Wahhab (1703–92) called, once again, for a return to the purer form of early Islam. The Saudi monarchy developed out of a 1745 alliance between al-Wahhab and the house of Saud, a partnership revived in 1932 by Abdul Aziz Ibn Saud, founder of modern Saudi Arabia. In return for a guarantee that the kingdom would be governed by sharia (Islamic) law, the reform cleric and his descendants would support the monarchy.[29] Although *Wahhabism* remained concentrated in Saudi Arabia, it did influence Egypt's Muslim Brotherhood, forerunner of both Islamic Jihad and al-Qaeda. The Saudi Monarchy made no effort to spread this brand of Salafism until the 1979 Islamic Revolution in Iran. Afraid that militant Shiite Islam would become the dominant force in the Muslim world, the Saudis launched an aggressive campaign to fund *Madrasas* (religious affiliated schools) in Sunni Muslim countries. These schools offered free education, books, and in some cases room and board. In countries such as Pakistan some, but by no means all nor even the majority, of these Madrasas would be a fertile recruiting ground for al-Qaeda.

Osama bin Laden and many of the Afghan Arabs belonged to the Wahhabi sect, and they in turn radicalized others. The Afghan jihad against the Soviets gave rise to a more extremist form of Salafism, *Jihadist-Salafism*.[30] Al-Qaeda embraced the early Salafist teaching that permitted rebellion against Muslim rulers who did not govern according to the correct teachings of Islam and the Salafist doctrine allowing them to declare other Muslims heretics. Bin Laden and his followers also made the lesser jihad a central rather than a peripheral teaching of their religion. Finally, they rejected the Prophet's distinction between combatants and noncombatants.

Situating the terrorists' ideology within its larger religious context is crucial to understanding and combating it. Wahhabism is the Saudi version of the larger Salafism, which has always been a minority movement within Islam. Contemporary Wahhabism permits neither rebellion against Muslim rulers nor declaring other Muslims heretics. Most Wahhabis do not advocate violence or condone terrorism. Jihadist-Salafism represents an even smaller subset of the Salafist movement. Islamism, on the other hand, embraces a much broader range of ideologies, including Salafism. This movement, sometimes called "the New Islamic discourse" espouses some beliefs that al-Qaeda has appropriated . Broadly speaking, Islamists wish to be governed by some form of sharia, reject western socialism and nationalism as organizing principles for Muslim states, support the complementarity but not the equality of the sexes, and deeply resent Western (and in particular American) interference in Muslim affairs.[31]

This commonality explains why so many Muslims responded to 9/11 by saying that although they condemned the terrorist attack, they understood its motives. Islamism creates a potentially sympathetic environment in which the extremists can operate. Without a large group of people who support their goals, even if they reject their methods, the terrorists would have no room to operate. The anti-abortion movement in the United States offers a useful comparative example. A significant number of Catholics and Protestants consider abortion morally wrong. A small subset of that group actively works to make abortion illegal. A very small percentage of those activists would damage facilities used to perform abortions, and only a tiny fraction of that group would condone taking the life of a doctor who performs abortions. *However*, without the larger group that shares their goal (however much they may disapprove their methods), the extremists would probably not be motivated or able to act.

The moderate Islamists (like legitimate anti-abortion groups) cannot be held responsible for the behavior of the extremists, although they arguably have a moral responsibility to speak out against them. Those opposing terrorism, however, must recognize the shared values of moderates and extremists, for only by doing so can they hope to separate the two. Dismissing al-Qaeda's ideology as merely "bad Islam" as opposed to the "good Islam" embraced by the vast majority of Muslims will not help in this ideological struggle.[32]

Conclusion

The 9/11 attacks left most Americans stunned and asking why al-Qaeda bore such hatred of the United States. The question prompted widely accepted but grossly oversimplified answers. Belief that the organization and its followers simply detest the American way of life gained wide acceptance. This belief in turn reinforced an already prevalent image of an irrational, anti-modern Islam, inherently prone to violence. These popular assumptions obscure the complexity of the terrorist ideology and the broader Islamist movement from which it draws inspiration.

Al-Qaeda pursues immediate political objectives in support of a long-term vision. It seeks the removal of secular and apostate regimes in the Muslim world and their replacement by Islamic republics governed by sharia law. The organization and its supporters targeted Egypt and Saudi Arabia in particular and attacked the United States for supporting them. These attacks, first against American interests abroad and finally against the American homeland, began only after the United States deployed troops to the Persian Gulf to repel the Iraqi invasion of Kuwait and then left many of them deployed in the region, including forces stationed in the sacred "land of the two mosques" (Saudi Arabia), long after. Frustrated that they could not achieve their political objectives in the Middle East because of American meddling, the terrorists saw no alternative to forcing U.S. withdrawal form all Muslim countries. American support for the state of Israel provides Osama bin Laden with a powerful example of a U.S. war against Islam, as does the occupation of Iraq. Replacing objectionable governments with Islamic ones, however, served a much broader ideological goal: reestablishing the uma or community of believers created by the Prophet Mohammed and his successors during the eighth century CE. In furtherance of this mission al-Qaeda wishes to cleanse Muslim lands of the immoral influences of Western secularism.

Al-Qaeda's broad ideological goals resonate with many people in the Muslim world who do not support its use of violence. Bin Laden and his followers represent an extreme manifestation of a broader Islamist reform movement. Contrary to popular belief, this movement does not simply reject modernity in favor of a utopian vision of a lost golden age. It seeks instead Muslim solutions to the challenges of the contemporary world, particularly an Islamic alternative to Western secular democracy.

CHAPTER 6

How Safe Are We?

Prevailing Myths

Prior to 9/11, many Americans had a naïve sense of security compounded by an offensive feeling of entitlement as to what life owed them in prosperity and happiness. The feeling of entitlement has survived, but a deep anxiety has replaced the sense of security. An exaggerated fear, at times deliberately manipulated for political gain, has convinced the average person that he or she stands at greater risk of becoming a victim of terror than he or she probably does. Since the majority of Americans lived a good portion of their lives under the Cold-War threat of nuclear annihilation, this exaggerated fear seems misplaced. Something about terrorism makes it far more personal and, therefore, terrifying. The Soviets aimed to kill *us*, but the terrorists want to kill *me*. The Cold War has had one lingering effect relevant to terrorism. Americans fear attack by weapons of mass destruction (nuclear, chemical, and biological) more than they fear any number of 9/11's, even though these weapons pose less of a threat than conventional weapons.

Exaggerated fear has given rise to an even more naïve belief: that the American homeland can someday be made completely secure from attack. A sobering assessment of the vulnerabilities of a country as vast, diverse, and globally connected as the United States reveals the absurdity of the absolute-security myth. This conclusion does not, however, mean that nothing can be done to make the country safer from terrorist attacks (as well as other threats). Assessing the nation's vulnerabilities within the context of the actual risk of terrorist attack makes the challenge of homeland security a bit less daunting. At the end of the day, however, Americans must face the uncomfortable truth accepted by every previous generation. Living in a free and open society entails risks that can be managed but not avoided. Only by acknowledging this simple fact, assessing the real (as opposed to the imagined) threat dispassionately, and then engaging in a rational cost-benefit analysis can we use our finite security resources wisely to improve our collective and individual security.

The Challenge of Homeland Security

The sheer size of the United States presents enormous security challenges. With an area of 5,984,684 square miles, the country is two and a half times the size of the European Union. It has an almost completely open border with Canada 5,526 miles long, a more tightly controlled but by no means secure border with Mexico 1,952 miles long, and 12,380 miles of coastline.[1]

Adding demographic data to the geographic picture compounds the challenge exponentially. By 2002 approximately 475 million people and 142 million cars, trucks and other vehicles were crossing American borders annually, while legally traded goods came through 3,700 terminals in 301 points of entry each day.[2] Customs figures for the single crossing between Windsor, Ontario and Detroit, Michigan for the year 2000 illustrate the enormous challenge of border security. In that year, 5,000 trucks per day entered the United States from Canada through customs facilities that allowed for an average inspection time of only two minutes per truck without causing a serious traffic jam.[3] An estimated 10.3 million undocumented workers lived in the United States as of April 2005, a 23% increase over the previous four years. As many as 800,000 people enter the United States illegally each year, 57% of them from Mexico alone.[4] These figures clearly indicate that despite a concerted effort to improve it, border security has been at best marginally effective.

Within those long open borders lies a vast, target-rich environment. The U.S. rail net includes 141,051 miles of track. Oil pipelines extend for 151,664 miles and gas lines for 340,172 miles.[5] Add to this list of vulnerabilities millions of miles of electric and telephone lines, thousands of bridges and tunnels, power plants, generating stations, chemical and fuel tanks, etc. Public buildings, museums, art galleries, houses of worship, shopping malls, sports and entertainment venues, and virtually any large gathering of citizens provide even more potential terrorist targets.

The daunting challenges of homeland security can be addressed, but only by first defining what "security" actually means, then assessing risks and vulnerabilities, and finally deciding which of the most cost-effective security measures to take. "Security," defined as complete freedom from attack, can never be achieved. "Security," understood to mean reducing the risk of attack to an acceptable level and mitigating the consequence of incidents when they do occur, can be improved. Deciding on an "acceptable level of risk," however, requires facing some difficult questions. Citizens must first distinguish between how safe they actually *are* as opposed to how safe they *feel*. They can then decide how much safer they wish to become and consider how much they are willing to spend to reach that new level of security. This formula may be difficult to work out for a nation, but each of us confronts it every time we get into a car.

We understand the dangers of driving, take reasonable precautions to lessen them, see the benefits of the automobile, and then accept the risk of turning the ignition key. None of us drives a tank, which would be very safe, but few of us ride motorcycles. We wear seat belts, maintain our vehicles, avoid driving while tired or under the influence of alcohol, drugs or medications, and then take our chances on the road.

When it comes to the terrorist threat, the country as a whole should make a similar assessment. First, consider the level of threat. Then consider the potential for different types of terrorist attack. Decide what measures can be taken to reduce the risks. Consider the cost of implementing those measures, and finally decide whether the security each measure provides is worth that cost.

Risk Assessment

Insurance companies depend for their livelihood on accurate risk assessment. If they wish to profit from selling life insurance, they must collect more in premiums than they pay out in benefits. To accomplish this goal they must accurately figure the odds the average person faces of dying at a particular age. If they miscalculate, they will sell too many policies at insufficient premiums to high-risk clients and go out of business. The need for accurate information about the odds of dying gave birth to actuarial science, a discipline that collects and analyzes statistical data on causes of death. This data sheds a great deal of light on the real as opposed to the imagined risk the average American faces from terrorism.

In 2002, the National Safety Council assembled a comprehensive list of more than 100 causes of death due to injury and calculated the annual and lifetime odds of succumbing to them. Not surprisingly transportation accidents scored high, thanks to America's love affair with the automobile. The average American has a 1 in 228 lifetime chance of dying in an automobile, either as a passenger or as a driver. He or she has a 1 in 229 chance of being killed in an accidental fall, and a 1 in 1,179 chance of dying in a fire. The figures for violent crime reveal how good Americans are at killing one another without help from foreign terrorists. The odds of death from assault stand at 1 in 211, thanks to the high incidence of gun violence, which presents the average American with a 1 in 315 lifetime risk of being shot to death. The National Safety Council figures do not list "terrorist attack," which may be subsumed in the category, "war and sequelae" (war and its after effects). Compared to other causes of death, this risk ranks fairly low on the list, exposing the average American to a 1 in 1,310 chance of dying.[6] Other actuarial assessments have factored in terrorism. According to one such calculation, the lifetime odds of dying from a terrorist attack are 1 in 88,000 as opposed to a 1 in 55,928 chance of being killed by lightning.[7]

Although this data clearly indicate that terrorism ranks very low on the long list of things that kill Americans, it should be viewed with a certain caution. Risk to a nation cannot be measured entirely in terms of risk to individuals. The cost of terrorism in lives and dollars continues to rise, and the chance of a truly catastrophic attack (which 9/11 was not) remains. Still these numbers underscore an important truth: the average American stands far less chance of being a victim of terror than he or she probably believes. The risk of various types of terrorist threat must, however, be examined in order to further allay exaggerated fear and so that steps to reduce the threats can be considered.

The Conventional Threat

Despite the fear engendered by unconventional weapons, conventional attacks still pose the greatest threat. Terrorism analysts apply the term "conventional" to firearms, explosives, and indeed any weapons not classified as chemical, biological, or nuclear. The perpetrators of 9/11 used primitive conventional weapons, simple box cutting knives, to hijack airplanes and turn them into flying bombs aimed at buildings with devastating effect. The Madrid and London terrorists used conventional explosives. Car bombs in Baghdad also fall into the conventional category as do "improvised explosive devices" (IEDs), often bombs, artillery shells, or other ordinance detonated as roadside bombs

Technology has amplified the killing power of conventional weapons without changing their basic nature. Plastic explosives such as Semtex are stable and pliable, so they can be molded into any shape and easily hidden. Combined with an altimeter switch a Semtex bomb hidden in a tape player can easily destroy an airplane as it did Pan Am Flight 103 over Lockerbie, Scotland in 1988. Cell phones can also be used to detonate explosives from a safe distance as occurred in the Madrid train bombings. Fertilizer laced with racing fuel makes the devastating sort of bomb used by Timothy McVeigh and Terry Nichols in Oklahoma City in 1995.

Perhaps the greatest threat comes from a decidedly low-tech use of conventional explosives. Suicide bombers carrying backpacks or brief cases or wearing explosive vests can detonate them at a chosen target or sooner if they face capture. They can also drive a truck or car packed with explosives and detonate it at will. Appropriately dubbed "the poor man's cruise missile," the suicide bomber has proven very effective and incredibly difficult to stop. Individual bombers can easily board trains and buses, walk into buildings or crowds, and detonate their bombs. Barriers can keep car and truck bombs away from buildings but cannot stop individuals from entering those buildings.

Besides explosives anything that can be used to commit an ordinary murder can be employed to perpetrate an act of terror. Terrorists use guns and knives for assassinations. They might also go on a killing spree like the Washington sniper or perpetrate a single attack with semi- or fully automatic weapons as the two alienated teenagers did at Columbine High School in 1999 and Baruch Goldstein did in the Hebron mosque attack of 1994. Inexpensive firearms can be easily obtained in the United States, and some semi-automatic weapons can be converted to fully automatic weapons with a cheap, readily obtainable kit. Since terrorists seem to like explosions, which usually cause more casualties and greater damage, firearm attacks have not been their preferred modus operandi. This situation could change, however, if it becomes more difficult to perpetrate bombings.

Accelerants used to start fires could also be employed to deadly effect by terrorists. Inexpensive accelerants can be purchased at any gasoline station or hardware store. Fortunately, burning down steel and concrete buildings cannot be done very easily, and wood frame buildings do not normally contain the large numbers of people terrorists wish to kill. In addition, the United States has excellent fire prevention, detection, and fighting capability, particularly in public buildings. Terrorist have proven to be very imaginative, however, so no threat should be completely ignored. Ordinary fire prevention, detection, fighting, and investigation provide the best insurance against arson attacks.

Weapons of Mass Destruction (WMD)

Although the United States has yet to suffer a WMD attack, even the threat of such an attack worries security experts and terrifies ordinary people. The United States defines WMD as

> Weapons that are capable of a high order of destruction and/or being used in such a manner as to kill large numbers of people. Can be nuclear, chemical, biological, or radiological weapons but excludes the means of transporting or propelling the weapons where such means are a separable and divisible part of the weapon. Chemical Weapons and Biological Weapons need to be of a certain size to count as WMD—single chemical or biological artillery rounds would *not* be considered to be WMD, due to the limited damage they could produce.[8]

Each category of WMD poses a specific set of threats to be countered and consequences to be managed should an incident actually occur which must be considered.

Nuclear Weapons

Nuclear terrorism involves two scenarios: detonation of an actual fusion or fission weapon, or use of a radiological or dirty bomb. Although mounting a nuclear attack against an American city would be extremely difficult, the results of such an attack would be catastrophic. Even a small, crude nuclear device with 2/3 the yield of the Hiroshima bomb detonated at Grand Central Station in New York City would kill half a million people immediately, cause a trillion dollars worth of economic damage, and instigate widespread panic.[9] The first step in mounting such an attack would be acquiring either an existing weapon or the highly enriched uranium necessary to make one. Existing weapons, including "suitcase" nuclear bombs, might be acquired from the old Soviet arsenal, some of which was left unsecured and even went missing during the collapse of the Soviet Union. Nuclear weapons could also fall into terrorist hands if Islamist military personnel in Pakistan "donated" them or if the regime itself fell under control of extremists like the Taliban.[10] Weapons-grade uranium might be stolen from one of the more than 130 research reactors in 40 countries and used to make a bomb.[11] Such a device could then be smuggled into the country in a number of ways via a shipping container unloaded at a U.S. port, in a vehicle crossing long land borders, or via a small boat landing along open coastline. Efforts to deter such an attack focus on helping to secure the Soviet arsenal, protecting stores of weapons grade material around the world, preventing proliferation of nuclear weapons, and replacing highly enriched uranium reactors with ones using safer nuclear fuel.[12] Port and border security will be discussed in Chapter 7.

"Dirty" (radiological) bombs would be easier to make and deliver but have a less devastating effect than a nuclear bomb. However, their damage could still be considerably greater than that caused by even a large conventional bomb. Radiological bombs use conventional explosives to spread radioactive material like Cobalt 60 or Cesium 137 over an area of several hundred city blocks rendering it uninhabitable for as long as forty years unless a slow, costly clean up could be mounted (which would be by no means certain). Thousands would die of cancer in the months and years following the attack. Dispersal of less radioactive material or smaller amounts could still contaminate tens of blocks forcing immediate evacuation of the area, spreading panic and perhaps necessitating demolition of buildings that could not be decontaminated.[13] As with nuclear bombs, securing dangerous material offers the best hope of deterring such an attack. Unfortunately, radioactive material is far more abundant than weapons grade uranium. Acquiring it in sufficient quantity undetected would not be easy and handling it to make a bomb would put the terrorists themselves at risk. However, the seemingly inexhaustible supply of suicide bombers willing to die delivering conventional bombs suggests that volunteers for such a hazardous mission could be readily obtained.

Another scenario has terrorists using conventional explosives against a nuclear facility to cause a reactor meltdown such as the one that occurred by accident at Chernobyl in the Ukraine in 1986. In that accident, fewer than 100 people died within the first year as a result of radiation exposure, but cancer deaths directly attributable to the long-term effects of radiation may reach 4,000 for those with the highest exposure. The overall cancer rate for those receiving lesser doses of radiation may increase by 1%.[14] However, the impact of the accident went far beyond immediate or even long-term loss of life. Over 300,000 people had to be evacuated and much of the area around the plant remains uninhabitable.

In 2005 the National Academy of Sciences reported that terrorists could achieve similar results by bombing the pools used to cool and store spent nuclear fuel rods. A committee of the National Academy of Science Board on Radioactive Waste Management concluded "that an attack which partially or completely drains a plant's spent fuel pool might be capable of starting a high-temperature fire that could release large quantities of radioactive material into the environment." The committee recommended measures be put in place to continue cooling the rods using sprayers in the event the pools suffered damage.[15] Nuclear reactors also topped the list of targets to be protected from attack following 9/11.

Chemical Weapons

Chemical weapons have been in use for almost a century. They first appeared on the battlefields of the First World War as "mustard gas" (named for its distinctive yellow color) consisting of phosgene, chlorine, or other acidic mixture in gaseous form. The gas liquefied on contact with moist membranes of the eyes, nose, and lungs, burning, blinding, and causing death if inhaled in sufficient concentration. Conventional armies abandoned use of mustard gas primarily because it had little effect on battles, posed serious danger to their own troops, and became relatively useless once static trench warfare ended. Five types of chemicals have potential as lethal terrorist weapons: nerve agents, blister agents, choking agents, blood agents, and toxins. Mustard gas, which has already been discussed, provides the best example of a choking agent. Blister agents are named for their caustic properties, and toxins are fatal when ingested. Blood agents like hydrogen cyanide must be inhaled and kill by shutting down oxygen transport in the bloodstream. Nerve agents, most of which must also be inhaled, cause death by attacking the central nervous system and shutting down vital functions like breathing and heartbeat.[16]

Fortunately, chemical agents present serious problems that limit their effectiveness as terrorist weapons. Most pose considerable risk to the handler, and using many of them requires protective gear that would draw attention to the terrorists. Chemical agents have to be delivered in sufficiently high concentration to be fatal, and their effectiveness diminishes with time and distance from ground zero. Weather conditions affect gases to such a degree that terrorists would have to assume that as much 95% of the agent would not reach its target. For example, the Pentagon estimates that it would take 220 pounds of sarin released in the open air to kill 500 people.[17] Circulating nerve or other gas through a building ventilation system sounds easy but requires more than pumping the gas into an air shaft. Terrorists would require a sophisticated knowledge of the building and its ventilation system to get the right concentration of gas; temperature and humidity might impede effective delivery; and filtration could prevent it all together.[18] Poisoning a municipal water supply would require even greater quantities of a chemical, which might be rendered inert by water treatment or removed by filtrations systems at the plant and/or in consumer homes.

The most recent chemical attack illustrates both the potential threat of such terrorism and its limitations. In 1995 the Aum Shinrikyo cult released sarin nerve gas on the Tokyo subway. The attack killed surprisingly few people because the terrorists used a mixture of the gas too dense to circulate properly. The twelve people who died appear to have been knocked to the floor of the subway cars where they inhaled a fatal concentration of the gas. The attack injured over 1,000 others. The possibility that terrorists might find more effective agents or a better means of distributing them must be taken seriously, but in their present form chemical agents have been far less effective than conventional bombs.

A more plausible and troubling scenario than terrorist dispersal of chemical agents involves use of conventional explosives to turn industrial chemicals into a toxic cloud near a populated area. While no such terrorist attack has yet occurred, the industrial accident at the Union Carbide Plant in Bopal, India suggests what the consequences of such an attack might be. Tanks filled with liquid mercury in a facility near Belgrade, Serbia might have produced a toxic cloud that would have killed thousands of people had it been struck by errant bombs during the 1999 war. The Department of Homeland Security has wisely begun to focus on industrial security, although a great deal more must be done in this vital area.

Biological Weapons

Americans harbor an intense fear of bioterrorism based on an exaggerated and mistaken notion of the ease with which biological agents can be acquired and distributed. Spy novels and grade B movies offer fictional accounts of super bugs that spread rapidly, kill instantly, and resist treatment. Flawed studies, political grandstanding, and deliberate propaganda add to the paranoia. The best evidence suggests that while terrorists could use a biological weapon to kill an individual or even a small group, inflicting the mass casualties they desire would require access to material, technical expertise, and effective means of distribution they simply do not possess, at least for the present. According to a report issued by the Chemical and Biological Weapons Nonproliferation Project at the Henry L. Stimson Research Center, "To employ a disease—a natural killer—as a weapon of war is theoretically an alarmingly straightforward concept. However, effectively harnessing Mother Nature's killing capacity is, according to many an expert, easier said than done."[19]

Biological weapons are disease-causing pathogens in the form of bacteria or viruses or the toxins these pathogens produce. The Centers for Disease Control divides biological agents into three categories (A, B, C) based on ease of transmission, lethality, potential to cause panic, and need for special health care measures.[20] Fortunately, relatively few type A pathogens have much potential as terrorist weapons, and even those that do confront the user with serious challenges. The most rapidly transmitted and lethal germs cause diseases humanity has faced for thousands of years and for which it has developed preventive measures, remedies, and/or containment procedures. They include cholera, smallpox, plague, ebola, and botulism. Terrorists would need to acquire lethal strains of a pathogen, produce the germ in large quantities, and distribute bugs in sufficient concentration to kill large numbers of people—all without being detected. Pathogens are sensitive to temperature, humidity, sunlight, mechanical activity, pollutants, oxygen, and other environmental conditions hard enough to monitor in a laboratory and impossible to control outside of one.[21]

Modern science also provides significant resources to prevent, treat, and/or contain outbreaks, naturally occurring or terrorist induced. Vaccines deliberately introduce dead or weakened forms of the pathogen into the human body, stimulating its immune system to produce antibodies to the live germ and immunizing the recipient against infection. Antibiotics attack many disease-causing bacteria after a person becomes ill and, in some cases after exposure but before symptoms appear, although they have no effect on viruses. Good hygiene supplemented by additional precautions such as boiling water or washing fruits and vegetables with disinfectants commonly used in countries lacking potable water could also help to contain an outbreak. Quarantining infected people can prevent an attack from becoming an epidemic. A review of specific pathogens commonly considered potential WMDs further illustrates the difficulties of using biological weapons.

Cholera is a disease caused by water-born bacteria virtually eliminated as a threat in countries with good sanitation and safe drinking water and for which a vaccine exists. A vaccine also exists for the virus that causes smallpox, although it is not routinely administered in the United States, and the disease itself can be treated. Sanitation has eliminated plague in most western countries, and antibiotics kill the bacteria that cause it. Efforts to disseminate botulism in canned food or bottled milk would be hampered by pasteurization and food processing. The anaerobic bacterium that produces the deadly toxin dies on contact with the air and would be killed by thoroughly heating, for example, canned soup. Efforts to spread disease via municipal water distribution systems would be thwarted by filtration at the plant and in private homes and by water-treatment chemicals such as chlorine, which kills most pathogens.

The deadly virus Ebola, which causes Ebola Hemorrhagic Fever, first appeared in 1976 and has been confined so far to outbreaks in central Africa. Although highly lethal and difficult to treat, Ebola presents serious problems as a terrorist weapon. With virtually no incubation period, the virus cannot be easily transmitted by a carrier host. Since people become infected by contact with a sick person's blood or secretions, containing an outbreak in a developed society would be easier than containing infection from an airborne pathogen.[22] The speed with which the disease kills its victims also reduces its capacity to spread. Patients die before coming into contact with large numbers of people.

Smallpox has a somewhat greater potential as an effective bioterrorism agent, but it too presents problems. With its 7–16 day incubation period, it could be brought into the country undetected in the body of a "suicide host" and spread extensively before being detected; it has a 30% mortality rate.[23] Although the smallpox virus spreads via direct interpersonal contact and is generally not airborne, its long incubation period allows a single carrier to infect many people before realizing he or she even has the disease.[24] A smallpox outbreak can, however, be contained with reasonable quarantine measures and infected people treated. Scientists have created a virtual (computer generated) epidemic simulation of a bioterrorist attack on Portland, Oregon using smallpox. The study yields very reassuring results. Presuming that terrorists released the virus undetected, health officials would become aware of it ten days later when the first victims exhibited symptoms. If the government took no action, the attack would be devastating, infecting 23,919 people and killing 551 of them by day 35, and infecting 380,582 people of whom 12,499 would die by day 70. However, reasonable health measures would avert this catastrophe. A strategy of "targeted vaccination and quarantine" beginning on day 14 would reduce the number of infected people to 2,564, limit the number of fatalities to 312, and contain the outbreak by day 35 by vaccinating 29,910 people and quarantining 30,550. By day 70 no new cases would have appeared, another 123 people would have died, 6,815 more people would be quarantined and 6647 more vaccinated. The simulation revealed that containing the outbreak required early response, and that people voluntarily quarantining themselves by simply staying at home would have had the greatest single impact on halting the outbreak. A reasonable response strategy well within the capability of most American cities would have reduced the death toll from 12,499 to 435.[25]

Using a virulent pathogen like smallpox also poses enormous "blow-back" risks to the terrorists. An infected individual(s) could return to the terrorists' homeland, unknowingly carrying the disease. Poor sanitation, water treatment, and health care in most non-western countries would make the effects of an epidemic in them far more deadly than it would be in the United States. That risk, the difficulty of obtaining and deploying a pathogen, and its delayed effect in contrast with the concentrated, dramatic impact of a bomb blast make smallpox and other germs less than ideal weapons.

Anthrax has thus far shown the greatest potential as bioterrorism weapon. *Bacillus Anthracis* is a bacterium found in soil that normally infects animals. Humans usually get the disease from handling infected livestock. Anthrax infection takes three forms: cutaneous, gastrointestinal, and inhalation. In nature the spores clump into large particles too heavy to be airborne, so humans rarely suffer the more deadly inhalation anthrax. "Weaponizing" anthrax requires isolating a lethal strain (most found in nature would not suffice), breaking the clumps of spores into smaller particles (a few microns in diameter) and treating the particles with silicon or some other coating to prevent their clumping once more. The weaponized anthrax can then be dried and stored or transported as a powder that can be easily hidden and safely handled with reasonable precautions. To have greatest impact, the attackers would need to aerosol the particles (put in them in a solution that could be sprayed) for dispersal against a target population.[26] Breathed in sufficient concentration the spores kill rapidly with untreated mortality rates approaching 100%. They then settle to the ground and either die or become inert.

These characteristics led the United States and the Soviet Union to develop anthrax as a biological weapon for use in conventional war. The pathogen could be rapidly dispersed, would quickly kill the enemy, and would then lose its potency, allowing troops to advance through targeted areas with little risk of infection. Although anthrax cannot be easily refined, stockpiles of weapons-grade pathogens probably still exist in the old Soviet arsenal and possibly in a handful of other countries suspected of having biological weapons programs. Not knowing what stocks of weaponized anthrax even exist and who has them adds to the general anxiety. However, in its 2001 report on compliance with and adherence to international conventions on arms control, the U.S. Department of State could say with confidence that only three nations, Iraq, China, and Russia, had active biological weapons programs. Since the 2003 invasion, no evidence of the Iraqi program, which may have been dismantled in the mid 1990s, has yet been found. The report describes Cuba, Iran, Libya, North Korea, and Syria as having the "expertise," "capability," or "potential" to make biological weapons.[27] Investigators later determined that Cuba and Libya had no such weapons programs.[28] Even if states have weaponized anthrax, they would be reluctant to give such pathogens to terrorists. Russia and China would almost certainly not do so, and the two remaining members of President Bush's "Axis of Evil," Iran and North Korea, have seen the consequences of American anger directed against the third, Iraq, a lesson that would not be lost on Syria either. Intelligence gathered following the invasion of Afghanistan has not produced any convincing evidence that al-Qaeda was even close to obtaining anthrax or any other pathogens.[29]

Assuming terrorists could acquire weapons-grade anthrax, delivering it in sufficiently lethal concentration over a wide area would be no easy matter. "The most efficient aerosolizations for BW [biological weapons] require considerable technological sophistication," concluded one pre-9/11 study of WMD, "and remain beyond the reach of most states and terrorists groups."[30] Crop dusters and pesticide sprayers have been suggested as delivery systems, but neither would be very effective. Dispersing anthrax from the air would require a precise and complex calculation of the concentration of spores in the liquid "slurry" put in the sprayer, and as many as 95% of the spores could be destroyed passing through the sprayer nozzle, which would also be prone to clogging. Environmental factors already noted (wind, sunlight, humidity, temperature, pollutants, etc.) could also adversely affect distribution. Sprayers available in most hardware stores do not generate small enough particle aerosols and/or have low throughput rates. Distributing anthrax through a building ventilation system presents similar difficulties.[31]

Even if terrorists do mount an effective attack with a particularly lethal strain of weaponized anthrax, the targeted population would not be helpless. Antibiotics can stop the disease even after exposure but not after the onset of symptoms. Inhalation anthrax is not normally contagious. A vaccine does exist but requires several doses and months to be effective, so it is generally administered only to those at extremely high risk of exposure to the pathogen. Americans can take considerable comfort from the one anthrax attack mounted against the United States. In an operation beginning a week after 9/11 and running through mid-October, terrorists sent weapons-grade anthrax through the mail, a crude system of delivery that killed only five people.[32] The attack had more psychological than lethal effect.[33]

Measures to prevent or at least decrease the likelihood of bioterrorism include controlling access to pathogens, stockpiling vaccines, and deploying detection equipment at strategic locations. Adequate supplies of up-to-date antibiotics used to treat an outbreak need to be maintained at points that enable rapid distribution. Since the possibility remains that someone will develop a more virulent pathogen and find an effective way to disperse it, scientific research to anticipate and counter such a threat must continue. Education and training of emergency responders and ordinary citizens may be the most effective measures of all. Gathering materials to create a sealed room in which to hide should an attack occur (as the Department of Homeland Security suggests) would, however, be a waste of time, energy, and duct tape.

Conclusion, Calculating the Risk and Counting the Cost

The size and openness of the United States make the country difficult to secure from terrorist attack. The vast, intricate infrastructure on which its citizens depend creates a target-rich environment for terrorists. The diversity of the American population allows foreign terrorists to blend in easily with the general population. Despite these vulnerabilities, however, Americans face less risk from terrorism than they imagine. Conventional weapons still pose the greatest threat, though the lethality of WMD makes them a serious concern. Nuclear attack, using either a nuclear or radiological bomb, would be difficult to mount but has the potential to be catastrophic. Chemical weapons thus far have proven less dangerous than conventional bombs. Bioterrorism also has the potential to inflict mass casualties, but it too cannot be easily carried out and poses serious risk to the terrorists themselves.

Considerable evidence suggests that the greatest threat WMD possess lies not in the casualties it would inflict but in the panic it might cause. The sarin gas attack on the Tokyo subway sent 5,000 people rushing to hospital emergency rooms, but only 1,000 of these "victims" showed any sign of having been exposed to the nerve agent. The anthrax attack on the United States produced extremely low casualties but panicked so many others into demanding prescriptions for cipro that a shortage of this valuable antibiotic occurred. The threat of chemical and particularly biological terrorism has been greatly, and in some cases deliberately, exaggerated either to justify vast spending on bio-defense or to keep people in a state of fear so that they can be politically manipulated. The best antidote to fear is good information. In the face of a seemingly endless list of threats Americans have two choices: become a hostage to their own anxiety or take reasonable precautions to reduce the risk of attack and preparations to mitigate the consequences of an incident when it does occur.

CHAPTER 7

Responses to Terrorism

Prevailing Myths

At times the terrorist threat seems so pervasive and persistent, and the vulnerabilities of a free, open, and complex society so great, that trying to achieve greater security seems like an exercise in futility. On other occasions the vast array of military and nonmilitary resources the United States and its allies can bring to bear on al-Qaeda suggest that it is only a matter of time before the scourge of terrorism is completely eradicated once and for all. Of course, neither conclusion is accurate. A threatened state can reduce the risk of terrorist attack, prepare appropriate responses for dealing with the consequences of an attack when (not "if") it occurs, and take offensive action (military and nonmilitary) against terrorist organizations and their supporters. Responses to terrorism fall into three broad categories, each of which contains general goals, specific objectives, and concrete measures. The North Atlantic Treaty Organization (NATO) has developed a useful concept, which has been adopted by the Pentagon, for organizing responses to terrorism.

Elements of Combating Terrorism

In the immediate aftermath of 9/11, NATO invoked Article 5 of the Washington Treaty (1949), the organization's founding document, proclaiming that al-Qaeda's attack on the United States was an attack on the alliance and its members. NATO then set about developing a "Military Concept for Defense against Terrorism." The Prague Summit Meeting of Heads of State (October 2002) approved the Concept, which the Pentagon has since adopted as official U.S. military doctrine. The Concept defines four broad tasks:

1. anti-terrorism to protect NATO forces, installations and personnel and to assist member nations in protecting their citizens and infrastructure from terrorist attack;

2. consequence management to aide member states in mitigating the effects of an actual terrorist attack;

3. counterterrorism to take offensive action against terrorist organizations, personnel, and facilities;

4. military cooperation with civilian institutions, government and private, to defend against terrorism.[1]

Although the Concept considers "cooperation" a core task, it is really a mechanism for carrying out the other three.

Drafted as a military doctrine, the NATO Concept nonetheless provides an excellent framework for organizing national responses to terrorism. Antiterrorism includes the specific objectives to secure the American homeland from attack. Consequence management consists of all measures taken at local, state, and national levels to prepare for and, when necessary, respond to an actual terrorist attack. Counterterrorism refers to offensive military and law enforcement operations against terrorist

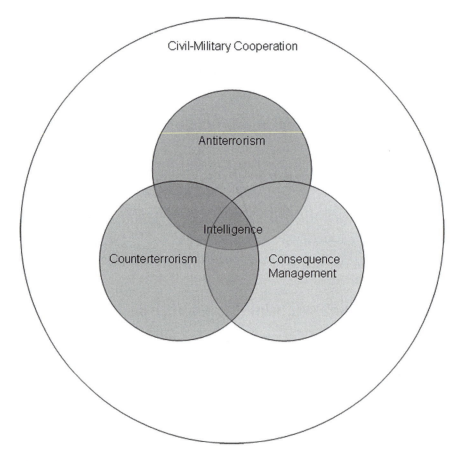

Figure 7.1: Elements of a comprehensive response to terrorism.

organizations, networks, and individuals at home and abroad along with economic, social, and diplomatic measures to attack the root causes of unrest that encourage terrorist activity. All three tasks require cooperation among a variety of civilian and military, governmental, and nongovernmental actors. Intelligence—the difficult task of gathering, analyzing, and sharing information—lies at the center of all three and helps tie them together (see Figure 7.1).

Antiterrorism

In addition to the death and destruction they caused, the 9/11 attacks administered a profound shock to the American psyche. Accustomed to extraordinarily high levels of personal and national security, Americans saw that they could be attacked anywhere and at any time. Fear of terrorism has made millions of people afraid to travel abroad, board aircraft, use mass transit, and attend large public gatherings. The terrorist attacks led to a broad range of measures under the broad heading of "homeland security." Most of these measures would be described as passive in that they aim to protect people, buildings, and other possible targets from attack rather than to pursue the terrorists.

Target Hardening

The United States took its first serious antiterrorism measures not after 9/11 but after the 1995 Oklahoma City bombing. The federal government, states, and municipalities began to "harden" high profile targets that they considered most prone to attack. Target hardening consists of measures taken to protect a building or facility from particular types of threat. Since truck bombs had been used against the World Trade Center (1993) and the Murrah Federal Building (1995), officials focused on that particular threat. They placed concrete barriers next to court houses, office buildings, and other prime targets and restricted parking next to such buildings. They also took steps to prevent people bringing bombs or weapons into these facilities. Metal detectors, which had long been a feature in schools and courthouses, became more common. Because terrorists loosely affiliated with the Christian Identity Movement perpetrated the Oklahoma City bombing, government buildings seemed the most likely targets. The 9/11 attacks further increased the emphasis on target hardening. Barriers now went up at museums, monuments, art galleries, and a host of other sites.

As public buildings have become better protected, privately owned structures have also received greater scrutiny. High-rise buildings in large cities seemed especially vulnerable after the collapse of the Twin Towers.

Most of the cost of hardening these buildings has fallen upon the owners, who understandably resist spending money that they cannot easily recover, especially when clients have become nervous about renting space in sky scrapers like Chicago's Sears Tower or Hancock Building. Given the impossibility of protecting everything, deciding which buildings to harden can be challenging. Securing one building often produces "target displacement," encouraging terrorists to move on to the next, "softer" target.

Transportation

The al-Qaeda attacks of course revealed that target hardening of strategic buildings, though important, had only begun to address the nation's vulnerabilities. Given the nature of the 9/11 attacks, airport security topped the list of anti-terrorist priorities. A host of measures addressed vulnerabilities revealed by the hijackings. Baggage and passenger screening improved, reinforced cockpit doors protected flight crews, and the number of air marshals increased on both international and domestic flights. Access to gates, baggage handling areas, and flight lines has been more restricted.

Airline security, however, means more than hardening individual airports. Collection of accurate passenger data by authorities abroad and its prompt transmission to the destination airport further contributes to homeland security. In May 2004, for example, the European Union and the United States reached an agreement on exchange of passenger name-record data.[2] The United States also monitors security at overseas airports and warns American passengers of facilities that do not meet U.S. standards.

While air security has improved dramatically since 9/11, protection of other transportation systems has not kept pace. The bombings in Madrid (2004) and London (2005) revealed the vulnerability of mass transit networks. Subways, commuter trains, and buses in all major American cities remain largely unprotected, primarily because relatively little can be done to make them safe. Despite years of experience fighting the Provisional Irish Republican Army, which frequently attacked the London Underground, the British could not prevent the July 7, 2005 attacks. Surveillance cameras aided the subsequent investigation of the incident and good crisis response mitigated its consequences, but neither could prevent the attacks. With so many access points to a commuter network that millions of people use each day, it remains to be seen how much can be done to achieve greater security. Users can be educated to report suspicious behavior and unattended packages, solid-walled trash cans in which explosives can be hidden may be removed, and undercover agents can be randomly assigned to trains. Given the diversity of people who ride trains and buses, however, including the homeless and those suffering mental illness, determining suspicious behavior can be quite tricky. Surveillance cameras may alert authorities to terrorists conducting dry runs prior to an actual attack, and they certainly help with the subsequent investigation following an incident, but they do not appear to deter terrorists, especially suicide bombers. Americans, furthermore, resist use of surveillance cameras as an intrusion on their privacy.

In July 2004, the Transportation Security Administration conducted a trial screening of passengers for explosives on Connecticut's Shoreline East rail line. Passengers boarding the train from eight trial stations passed through a special screening car that checked them for explosives while the train continued on its route. The Transportation Safety Administration also tested the effectiveness of AMTRAK baggage screening at Union Station that same month.[3] The limited scope of the tests, the sheer size of the American rail net, and the cost of such high-tech measures do not bode well for their effective use on a significant scale in the foreseeable future. The Homeland Security Organization, created to assist the Department of Homeland Security, has studied the problem of protecting mass transit. Most of their recommendations involve monitoring of stations, preventing unauthorized access to baggage, equipment, and control areas, and improved transit policing.[4] How to screen and monitor passengers remains a big question. While a few reasonable, cost-effective security measures may reduce slightly the likelihood of an attack on trains and subways, mass transit will remain vulnerable to attack for the foreseeable future. This sobering realization does not, however, mean that the consequences of such an attack cannot be effectively managed.

Maritime Security

Few areas of homeland security worry experts more than the relatively open access to the United States through its ports. Container security in particular presents the biggest challenge. Approximately half of world trade (by value) and 90% of general cargo travels the globe in closed metal containers the size of semi-trucks.[5] While many of these containers hold cargo packed at a single secure location, other boxes consist of small shipments consolidated to save cost. They can be loaded on a ship at one port, transferred to another vessel at a different location, and then cross the United States to their destination without being opened or inspected. As of 2002, the United States received 21.4 million container shipments annually.[6] Terrorists could use containers to smuggle in conventional explosives, a nuclear weapon, or terrorists themselves.

In addition to the cargos that they carry, the ships themselves pose a potential terrorist threat. "Terrorists can also take advantage of a vessel's legitimate cargo, such as chemicals, petroleum, or liquefied natural gas, as the explosive component of an attack."[7] The large number of storage tanks surrounding port facilities and the fact that some produce toxic chemicals when ignited would magnify the destruction caused by such a conventional detonation. Other maritime terrorist scenarios include use of hijacked ships to ram bridges, port facilities or other ships, use of speedboats loaded with explosives to attack vessels like the Cole, and the use of ships as missile launch platforms.[8]

Effective maritime antiterrorist measures can be very expensive and difficult to implement, adding high costs to a shipping industry often marginally profitable at best. Funding for port security has increased 700% since 9/11, rising from $259 million in fiscal year 2001 to $1.6 billion in 2006. The money funds additional customs and security personnel, bomb-sniffing dogs, and hi-tech gamma- and x-ray screening machines that can see into containers without opening them. The 2007 budget contains $157 million for next-generation detection equipment.[9] However, thoroughly screening each container takes time and more equipment than is currently available. While the percentage of containers screened with gamma- or x-ray equipment is not public information, it probably represents a fraction of the total. "Smart containers" with computerized locks have also been tested but have yet to be widely used, probably because of cost.

Securing American ports represents only one part of a broader maritime security strategy. Ideally, access to containers and the ships that carry them should be tightly monitored from point of origin to final destination. Under a "Container Security Initiative" the United States has the right to inspect "high-risk" cargo in 42 foreign ports with another 8 expected to join by the end of 2006.[10] Ships from ports in countries that refuse to participate in the program may be required to halt offshore while U.S. customs officials inspect their cargo. Other maritime antiterrorism measures include improved tracking of vessels on the high seas, timely exchange of information and intelligence between trade partners, and financial and training assistance to countries that lack the resources to improve port security on their own.[11]

Critical Infrastructure

"Critical infrastructure" refers to the networks and systems the nation requires to function, for lack of a better term—its economic, social, and political backbone. Critical infrastructure includes (but is not limited to) energy generation and delivery systems; water and sanitation facilities; financial systems; information networks and systems; food production and delivery; certain industrial facilities; and the health care system. Trade and transportation can be considered part of the national critical infrastructure but may also be treated as a separate category.

Critical infrastructure facilities such as power generating stations, water treatment and distribution plants, and communication centers can be protected by target hardening. Parking within a bomb-blast radius can be restricted, access to a facility controlled, and surveillance equipment installed. Networks and systems cannot be as easily defended with such measures. Protecting every mile of railroad track, oil pipe, and electric line would be impossible. Anti-terrorism measures should instead focus on rapid detection of attacks and quick restoration of services. Sensors in train tracks can reveal when a rail has been moved. Oil pipelines can be fitted with similar sensors and shut-off valves. A terrorist attack at one point in the line could be quickly identified and contained and response teams dispatched to apprehend the attackers and repair the damage. Terrorist may find cutting power lines relatively easy to accomplish but not very effective. Even the smallest communities face intermittent line breaks, usually caused by storms, and have the ability to deal with them quickly.

Information-dependent systems must be protected in yet another way. The American banking and financial networks depend on computers, which makes them susceptible to "cyber-terrorism." Cyber-terrorism includes "infecting" computer networks with viruses and worms to impede or halt their normal operations and gaining unauthorized access to sensitive, secret, or confidential information. Firewalls, anti-virus software, and other hi-tech strategies can be employed to prevent or counter cyber-terrorism. Frequent backing up of data and redundant storage and communication systems can also protect information-dependent systems.

Protecting critical infrastructure in the public domain challenges local, state, and federal governments, but those governments at least have considerable control over such assets and must answer to the voters if they fail to protect them. In America's free-market economy, however, 85% of critical infrastructure is in the private sector.[12] Motivated by profit and reluctant to incur costs that will reduce it, business and industry have been less willing to implement expensive antiterrorism measures without a legal requirement to do so and compensation. Tax incentives and insurance reductions may help, but progress in the private sector has been considerably slower than in the public. As the memory of 9/11 recedes over time, it may become even more difficult to require or even encourage protective measures of privately owned industries that use toxic chemicals in the course of normal operation, bio-labs, utilities, and other vital facilities and services.

In summary, antiterrorism presents massive challenges. The sheer size and complexity of the American social-economic system makes it very vulnerable to attack as does its increasing dependence on technology. Protecting everything is impossible and would not be cost effective even if it were. Only a careful, comprehensive and ongoing assessment of threats and vulnerabilities will enable the United States to make wise decisions about antiterrorism measures. Even then terrorists will occasionally succeed in attacking the American homeland. Responding to such attacks when thy occur can, however, reduce the consequences of them.

Consequence Management

Responding effectively to a terrorist incident can mitigate its consequences; responding ineffectively can make the results of the attack even worse. "Consequence management" refers to the broad range of activities taken to counter the effects of an attack over time. The terms "crisis response" and "emergency management" usually refer to steps taken in the immediate aftermath of an incident. The British response to the London bombings (2005) provides an instructive example of consequence management. Police promptly cordoned off the effected area while the London Transit Authority stopped trains, re-routed buses, and notified motorists to avoid central London. Hospitals set up triage centers and prepared to receive the wounded. Suitably equipped rescue workers entered the Underground to remove the wounded. In conducting rescue and recovery operations, these highly trained professionals exercised great care to avoid contaminating the crime scene that would have to be investigated. Special Air Service (elite special forces) units moved into position in case they would be needed to deal with armed terrorists. Throughout the crisis the London Metropolitan Police remained in control of the operation and provided regular press briefings as information became available and could appropriately be released. Once the police determined that the threat had passed, transit workers concentrated on getting the commuter system up and running by that evening's rush hour. In the words of a city paper, London was "open for business."

Despite its general effectiveness, the British response to the July 7 bombing received serious criticism in a report by the London Assembly published almost a year after the incident. Communications problems comprised the bulk of the concerns raised in the report. Emergency responders could not communicate with the London Underground Network Control Center. Nor could they communicate with one another underground. Emergency responders took longer to assess the situation and declare an emergency at two of the Underground stations than they did at the third. Too many emergency responders relied on cell phones whose networks became congested during the crisis. A breakdown in communications in the London Ambulance Service hampered dispatch of an appropriate number of ambulances to each scene and the effective distribution of injured to different hospitals. Medical personnel did not keep accurate records on the wounded. The authorities also failed to control the incident sites as effectively as they might have. Many walking wounded simply left the area without being identified or interviewed. Finally, the bombings revealed a lack of capacity to respond with sufficient medical equipment.[13]

Different types of attack may require different responses and/or the services of different emergency responders. Local law enforcement supported by its state and federal counterparts as needed would normally maintain order and apprehend perpetrators. Special Weapons Assault Teams (SWAT) might be needed to apprehend or neutralize heavily armed terrorists still at large. Local firefighters could handle most explosions and fires, but hazardous materials units would be called upon in the event of a terrorist attack using chemical or biological agents or in the event of a fire or explosion releasing toxic fumes. Local paramedics and hospitals could handle the dead and wounded in most cases but would require support from state and regional emergency responders and health care providers in the event that an incident produced mass casualties.

Crisis response may last hours, days or weeks, but consequence management can last for months. Catastrophic attacks may have consequences that take a very long time to manage and require the services of different types of responders at each stage of recovery. Consequence management in response to hurricane Katrina continues a year after the storm. In those cases National Guard, reserve, or regular military units might be called in to augment the local response capacity. Except in very unusual circumstances such as the complete collapse of civil authority the military should remain in a supporting role with the civil power in charge of operations. Finally, an informed and educated citizenry also has a crucial role to play in consequence management. To avoid panic, government, private institutions, and businesses should educate and train citizens about what to do in the event of different types of attack.

Fortunately, the United States had an extensive consequence management capacity long before 9/11. Responding to an accident or a natural disaster does not differ fundamentally from responding to a terrorist incident, although the mix of responders and their tasks will vary with each situation. Developing an effective terrorist attack response capacity consists largely of augmenting existing agencies, institutions, and facilities. The Department of Homeland Security now emphasizes "all-hazards" crisis response and consequence management. Local, state, and federal governments should plan and train for the whole range of potential crises ranging from natural disaster (tornado, hurricane, forest fire, etc.) through accidents (chemical spill, fire at industrial site, etc.) to terrorist attacks of various types. Planning requires a sober assessment of threats and vulnerabilities, identification of response assets, and prioritizing of likely crisis scenarios. Repeated and constantly updated training exercises will improve the quality of consequence management.[14]

In planning and organizing all-hazards response, great care must be taken not to weaken ability to respond to one kind of crisis while improving capacity to respond to another. In the aftermath of hurricane Katrina critics have suggested that the ability of the Federal Emergency Management Agency to respond to natural disasters has been weakened by embedding the agency in the Department of Homeland Security in order to focus on the terrorist threat. An all-hazards approach to consequence management does not require compromising response capacity for one type of crisis in order to deal with another. Within a particular environment, however, some threats will be greater than others and planning, education, and training should proceed accordingly.

In December 2005, the Department of Homeland Security published a *National Response Plan*, "an all-discipline, all-hazards plan that establishes a single, comprehensive framework for the management of domestic incidents." The *Plan* also "provides the structure and mechanisms for the coordination of federal support to state, local, and tribal incident managers and for exercising direct federal authorities and responsibilities."[15] The *Plan* operates under the reasonable assumption that the primary response to an incident of any kind will be local and that the federal government should be prepared to augment local capabilities and coordinate the response as needed.

Counterterrorism

In popular parlance, counterterrorism means all measures taken to combat the terrorist threat. In NATO and Pentagon doctrine, however, the term refers more specifically to offensive actions against terrorist organizations, networks, sponsors and individuals. Counterterrorism includes a broad spectrum of responses from conventional war against states that harbor or sponsor terrorists through law enforcement to arrest terrorists within the country. While antiterrorism is largely passive and consequence management reactive, counterterrorism is decidedly proactive.

Military

In the immediate aftermath of 9/11 counterterrorism focused on conventional military operations against state sponsors of terrorism. The United States, with the support of its NATO allies, invaded Afghanistan in late 2001 and removed the Taliban regime from power. Military operations have continued since the occupation, especially in the remote areas bordering Pakistan. Whether or not the 2003 invasion of Iraq had anything to do with counterterrorism in the first place, it clearly does now as al-Qaeda operatives entered the country in the aftermath of the invasion and have fought coalition and Iraqi security forces ever since. Counterinsurgency and counterterrorism operations will continue in that country for the foreseeable future.

Below the level of conventional war, the U.S. military conducts covert operations alone or in cooperation with allies. Details on such operations, of course, remain classified. The Pentagon does publicly acknowledge that it has disrupted ten terrorist plots since 9/11, three aimed at the United States and seven set to take place overseas. Terrorists had planned to use hijacked airplanes against West Coast targets in 2002 and East Coast targets the following year. In May 2002 Jose Padilla was apprehended at O'Hare International Airport in Chicago, suspected of plotting to blow up apartment buildings and perhaps to detonate a "dirty" (radiological) bomb. Information in the public domain indicates only that the these plots were disrupted but does not provide any precise details on how they were foiled. Certainly customs and law enforcement officials must have been involved in the domestic sting operations. The overseas plots targeted the United Kingdom, Pakistan, ships in the Straits of Hormuz, and an undisclosed American "tourist site" abroad. Details on these operations and the possible role of U.S. forces in carrying them out remain classified.[16]

In addition to direct action, the U.S. military contributes to counterterrorism through training and assistance programs in allied nations around the world. Run through the Office of Defense Cooperation located in many U.S. Embassies, these programs provide academic and practical instruction in combating terrorism. Other military assistance programs run through other Department of Defense offices and agencies provide tactical training and other assistance directly to foreign militaries. Similar assistance programs train, educate, and in some cases equip law enforcement agencies in friendly countries.

The Central Intelligence Agency (CIA)

Most Americans identify the CIA with intelligence gathering and analysis of security related information or "intelligence." The Agency has, however, always had an operational side. Covert operations remain highly classified, so it is usually not possible to do more than speculate about their extent and effectiveness. During the invasion of Afghanistan, CIA teams worked closely with the Northern Alliance to fight the Taliban. They acted as forward air controllers, directing air attacks against enemy positions, interrogated prisoners, and performed other military and paramilitary activities in the country. While the agency's intelligence gathering and analysis mission came under intense scrutiny after 9/11, its covert operations have not received such attention. Presumably the CIA continues to mount counterterrorism operations as opportunities present themselves.

Law Enforcement

As al-Qaeda has evolved into a highly decentralized global network, combating it has become increasingly a job for law enforcement. The Federal Bureau of Investigation (FBI) in cooperation with state and local police and other federal agencies (Alcohol, Tobacco, Firearms and Explosives; U.S. Citizenship and Immigration Services; U.S. Customs and Border Protection; etc.) leads the domestic counterterrorism effort. The FBI maintains Joint Terrorism Task Forces in 100 American cities, including at least one in each of 52 field offices, coordinated and directed by the National Joint Terrorism Task Force at FBI Headquarters in Washington. Since 9/11 the FBI has quadrupled the number of personnel assigned to the Joint Terrorism Task Forces, staffing them with "2,196 Special Agents, 838 state/local law enforcement officers, and 689 professionals from other government agencies (the Department of Homeland Security, the CIA, and the Transportation Security Administration, to name a few)."[17] The FBI also operates a Counterterrorism, Terrorist Screening Center with a 24-hour hotline. The center maintains the government's "Consolidated Terrorist Watch List," collects information, and assists law enforcement in identifying terrorists.[18]

The FBI has conducted a number of successful undercover and sting operations since 9/11. On September 13, 2002, agents from the Buffalo Field Office apprehended a six-member al-Qaeda cell in the Yemeni neighborhood of Lackawanna. All six had attended training camps in Afghanistan. Their precise role and/or mission has either not been determined or the information remains classified. The following year the FBI rounded up another six-member cell in Portland, Oregon. The Bureau has also disrupted terrorist financing activities and apprehended numerous terrorist suspects. It has dramatically expanded its counterterrorism capability by creating specialized units, both deployable and at FBI headquarters.[19]

To aid law enforcement in fighting terrorism, Congress passed the "USA Patriot Act" in October 2001 and renewed it with revisions in 2006. The Act expanded surveillance powers and the scope of certain warrants to gain access to a wide variety of electronic, voice, and telephone communication. The act loosened restrictions on information sharing between law enforcement organizations and government agencies and allowed for rapid seizure of terrorist assets in the United States It also contains numerous provisions on banking, immigration, border control, and criminal activities.[20] The law has been understandably controversial with civil libertarians who helped to get it amended when it came up for renewal in 2006.

Terrorist Financing

Stopping or at least reducing the flow of money to terrorist organizations can hamper their ability to conduct attacks. While turning off the money faucet sounds good in theory, it proves hard to accomplish in fact. Al-Qaeda and its affiliates have funded themselves through legitimate business activities, charitable front organizations (whose contributors may or may not know to whom their money really goes), direct contributions, criminal activity (drug smuggling, racketeering, extortion, etc.), and at one time Osama bin Laden's personal fortune. Since 9/11 the United States has concentrated on freezing the assets of known terrorists, shutting down suspect charities, and enforcing tougher bank reporting laws. The efficacy of such measures remains the subject of heated debate. While the administration often boasts of the millions of terrorist dollars seized or frozen, it cannot say what percentage of total terrorist assets this amount represents, let alone specify the capacity of the terrorist organizations to raise more money. Efforts to interdict the money supply founder through lack of international cooperation and the sheer scope of the task. Terrorists respond to tighter U.S. banking regulation by shifting operations to areas of the world with more lax laws and/or weaker enforcement.[21]

The relatively low cost of terrorist operations makes efforts to cut off funds even more problematic. Estimates for the cost of the 9/11 attacks, by far the most expensive al-Qaeda operation to date, go as high as $500,000. The Madrid train bombings cost around $50,000, and the London attacks perhaps as little as $12,000.[22] With the exception of 9/11, terrorist attacks can be funded locally through private donation or criminal activity. Reducing the ability of terrorist organizations to move money internationally may have the desirable effect of forcing local cells to raise their own funds through crime, thus increasing their risk of detection and capture. Attacking terrorists' financing has not, however, reduced their ability to strike.

The enormous difficulties in regulating international finance, the ability of illicit organizations to find alternative sources of revenue, and the low cost of operations have led some analysts to question the wisdom of trying to freeze or seize terrorist assets. They argue instead for exploiting the intelligence value of financial transactions. Following rather than stopping the money may alert authorities to an impending attack and would certainly improve understanding of terrorist organizations.[23] Combining both strategies may be the best approach.

Intelligence

Over thirty years ago, British General and counterinsurgency expert Sir Frank Kitson wrote that defeating terrorists "consisted very largely in finding them."[24] His wisdom remains sound. Intelligence, the collection and timely analysis of information on the terrorists' organization, plans, and whereabouts, remains central to counterterrorism. It also provides crucial information that can help prioritize antiterrorism measures. Consequence management, which includes criminal investigation and, if possible, apprehension of perpetrators, can generate intelligence that helps with counterterrorism operations. The U.S. intelligence community, consisting of some fifteen different agencies, came under intense scrutiny and significant criticism by the 9/11 Commission. The major intelligence breakdown lay not in failing to gather the necessary information on the impending attacks, but in failing to analyze and assemble the data into a coherent picture of the threat. The Commission highlighted the need for "unity of effort across the foreign-domestic divide," and called for removal of prohibitions barring the CIA and FBI from sharing information.[25]

To remedy the problems raised by the Commission, Congress passed the Intelligence Reform and Terrorism Prevention Act (IRTPA). The act created the Office of the Director of National Intelligence (ODNI) with a mandate to

> Collect, analyze, and disseminate accurate, timely, and objective intelligence, independent of political considerations, to the President and all who make and implement US national security policy, fight our wars, protect our nation, and enforce our laws. [26]

Overseen by the Director of National Intelligence, the ODNI coordinates and facilitates collection, analysis and sharing of intelligence among the country's intelligence agencies.

The ODNI also oversees the National Counterproliferation Center, which works to prevent proliferation of WMD, and the National Counterterrorism Center, "the primary organization in the United States Government (USG) for integrating and analyzing all intelligence pertaining to terrorism and counterterrorism (CT) and to conduct strategic operational planning by integrating all instruments of national power."[27] The National Counterterrorism Center serves largely as a clearinghouse for information exchange and a conference center. It also

> operates as a partnership of organizations to include: Central Intelligence Agency; Department of Justice/Federal Bureau of Investigation; Departments of State, Defense, and Homeland Security; and other entities that

provide unique expertise such as the Departments of Energy, Treasury, Agriculture, Transportation, and Health and Human Services; Nuclear Regulatory Commission; and the US Capitol Hill Police. [28]

Whether the ODNI really improves intelligence gathering or merely serves to "layer another official on top of the director of central intelligence," as one critic of the *9/11 Commission Report* suggests, remains to be seen.[29] The National Intelligence Council, in existence long before 9/11, has representatives from various intelligence agencies tasked with providing "forward-looking assessments of national security issues—for senior US policymakers."[30] This coordinating body did not overcome interagency rivalry, turf battles, and other barriers to cooperation, and it remains questionable whether creating new bureaucracies will overcome them either. A recent study suggests that the Defense Intelligence Agency has emerged as the top body gathering more assets into itself and surpassing the CIA.[31]

Conclusion

Responses to terrorism fall roughly into three broad task categories. *Antiterrorism* measures protect targets from attack. *Consequence management* prepares for and deals with the results of an incident and includes immediate crisis response and longer-term measures. *Counterterrorism* takes the fight to the terrorists with offensive military activities, covert operations and law enforcement efforts. Ideally, comprehensive and coordinated intelligence activity guides all three tasks and helps link them together. To be truly effective, however, these tasks need to be combined into a comprehensive plan, a grand strategy combining various elements of national power to defeat al-Qaeda.

Since 9/11 the United States has made a considerable effort to improve national security. Antiterrorism measures include hardening potential targets and protecting critical infrastructure. Crisis management has been enhanced to include responding to terrorist attacks as part of an all-hazards response approach. Like all preventive measures, the effectiveness of these improvements will only be known when they are tested.

Counterterrorism operations have embroiled the U.S. military in Afghanistan and Iraq. Law enforcement agencies have apprehended terrorists and prevented attacks at home and improved cooperation with their counterparts in other countries. The American intelligence community has been overhauled to improve collection, analysis, and information sharing. Congress created the Department of Homeland Security to coordinate the struggle against terrorism within the United States. Whether these measures represent different aspects of a comprehensive strategy or a series of ad hoc responses will be considered in Chapter 8.

CHAPTER 8

A Comprehensive Approach

Prevailing Myths

The impressive array of measures, tactics, and responses outlined in the previous chapter would seem to make a compelling case that the United States is waging an effective campaign against terrorism. New laws, new terrorism centers, new international agreements, millions if not billions of dollars spent on a broad array of responses surely add up to a solution to the al-Qaeda problem. And yet after five years and two wars, Osama bin Laden remains at large, and al-Qaeda and its affiliates still have the ability to mount operations as witnessed in Madrid and London. The number of Americans who have died in Afghanistan and Iraq rapidly approaches the death toll for 9/11 with no end to either war in sight. Any number of individual measures, no matter how worthwhile, do not an effective strategy make. The time has come to reexamine the current approach to countering the al-Qaeda threat and to consider alternatives.

Is there a Global War on Terrorism?

On the very day America sustained the worst terrorist attack in its history, Rep. Brad Sherman of California declared to the House of Representatives, "We . . . must wage a war against terrorism, [and] all terrorist groups."[1] Three days later Congress resolved

That the President is authorized to use all necessary and appropriate force against those nations, organizations, or persons he determines planned, authorized, committed, or aided the terrorist attacks that occurred on September 11, 2001, or harbored such organizations or persons, in order to prevent any further acts of international terrorism against the United States by such nations, organizations or persons.[2]

On September 20, 2001, nine days after the devastating attacks, President George W. Bush addressed a joint session of Congress and a stunned nation. "Our war on terror," he declared, "begins with al-Qaida, but it does not end there. It will not end until every terrorist group of global reach has been found, stopped, and defeated." He warned that the war would be long and difficult, that it would be unlike any other conflict in American history, and that the United States would suffer casualties.[3] There could be no doubt about it: the Global War on Terrorism (GWOT) had been declared, and the vast majority of Americans supported the declaration. Since September 20, 2001, analysts, scholars, and ordinary people have questioned whether the GWOT provides an adequate response to terrorism. Can a protracted struggle with an elusive enemy in a decentralized network throughout at least 60 countries be considered a war? More importantly, does the GWOT define the appropriate response to terrorism?

In September 2001 the GWOT may have made sense. The country had suffered a devastating attack, and the President needed to mobilize public support for a sustained struggle. The first round of hostilities had to be a conventional attack against the nation of Afghanistan, whose Taliban government sheltered bin Laden, allowed him to train on its soil, and supported him in other ways. A declaration of war, even a symbolic one, would ensure that Congress provided the resources necessary to conduct the conflict. Even America's allies in the North Atlantic Treaty Organization agreed with the decision to invade Afghanistan. "We consider the events of 11 September to be an armed attack not just on one ally, but on us all, and have therefore invoked Article 5 of the Washington Treaty," declared a ministerial meeting of NATO's governing body, the North Atlantic Council. "Accordingly, we have decided to support, individually and collectively, the ongoing US-led military operations against the terrorists who perpetrated the 11 September outrages and those who provide them sanctuary."[4] The UN Security Council unequivocally condemned the attacks and acknowledged "the inherent right of individual or collective self-defense in accordance with the Charter."[5]

Since the defeat of the Taliban, however, the GWOT has become increasingly problematic. As a metaphor for sustained struggle, a "war on terrorism" might have the same utility as a "war on poverty" or a "war on crime." However, the White House insists that the country has been in a real war since 9/11 and continues to use the state of war to justify extraordinary (perhaps even extralegal) measures employed to wage it. This assertion raises an immediate concern. A declaration of war requires some understanding of what constitutes victory. What does winning the GWOT actually mean? Addressing the Warsaw Conference on Combating Terrorism in November 2001, the President proclaimed that the United States "will not rest until terrorist groups of global reach have been found, have been stopped, and have been defeated."[6] Two years later the *National Strategy for Combating Terrorism* began by quoting that address but set a more modest goal of securing "a world in which our children can live free from fear and where the threat of terrorist attacks does not define our daily lives."[7] Since virtually every terrorist group has some degree of "global reach," even this vision of the future looks blurry. Without a clear definition of victory in the GWOT, the United States risks being locked in a permanent state of war. Use of the GWOT as an excuse for actions ranging from wiretapping without warrants to drilling for oil in the Alaskan wilderness raises further concerns over the appropriateness of a war on terrorism.

Insistence on "war" as an appropriate response to terrorism poses practical problems as well as conceptual ones. To begin with, it is impossible to make war on "terror," which is a weapon, or "terrorism," which is an ideology. Terrorist networks and organizations can certainly be targeted but not entirely or even primarily by military units. In addition, a state of war poses legal problems that may impede cooperation between allies. German authorities captured Mounir El Motassadeq, a Moroccan national and suspected al-Qaeda member, in Hamburg and convicted him in March 2004 for complicity in the 9/11 attacks. Motassadeq's lawyers appealed the conviction on the grounds that witnesses in U.S. custody would have exonerated their client had they been allowed to testify. The United States insisted that as prisoners of war the witnesses would not be allowed to appear in a German court. Insisting that since their country was not at war, a German appeals court overturned the conviction on the grounds that denying the defendant's right to call witnesses prevented him from receiving a fair trial. The court did, however, uphold Motassadeq's conviction for being a member of a terrorist organization.

The GWOT continues to cause tension between the United States and friendly states around the world. Most Western European nations do not believe in a war on terrorism. The newly independent nations of Central and Eastern Europe pay lip service to the GWOT because supporting the United States brought them tangible benefits including NATO membership, which an American veto could have blocked, and much needed foreign and military aide. Whether people on the streets of Warsaw, Prague, Budapest, or Bucharest share their governments' enthusiasm for the GWOT appears doubtful. Many allies and nonaligned nations resent being told "Either you are with us, or you are with the terrorists."[8] Few governments or populations see political choices in such black and white terms. Many of our allies who gladly supported the United States in Afghanistan did not do so in Iraq. This decision hardly means that they stand "with the terrorists."

In addition to these problems the GWOT places far too much emphasis on the military in combating terrorism. This focus accorded well with the administration emphasis on attacking state sponsors of terrorism using conventional military force. Afghanistan clearly qualified as such a state sponsor. The case of Iraq has, of course, proved to be far less clear. Persuasive evidence for the claim that Saddam possessed weapons of mass destruction that could threaten the United States has yet to be offered, and no link between his regime and al-Qaeda can be demonstrated. Leaving aside the Iraq controversy, few if any "state sponsors" of terrorism remain. While Tehran's support for insurgents in Iraq seems rather clear, attacking Iran would probably accomplish very little and could destabilize the region even further. Beyond the ongoing missions in Afghanistan and Iraq, the potential for a conventional military response to al-Qaeda and its affiliates seems quite limited.

National Strategy for Combating Terrorism

The Global War on Terrorism has been guided, at least since February 2003, by the *National Strategy for Combating Terrorism*. The document defines victory in the GWOT as the creation of a future in which "Americans and other civilized people around the world can lead their lives free of fear from terrorist attacks and where the threat of terrorist attacks does not define our daily lives."[9] Victory will be achieved through a "4D strategy" implemented during a protracted conflict over many years. The United States must *defeat* terrorist organizations, *deny* them state sponsorship, *diminish* the root causes of terrorism, and *defend* the American homeland and U.S. citizens abroad. Each strategic goal includes several specific objectives.[10]

The first "D" includes three objectives presented as steps in a linear process. The United States must first "identify," then "locate," and finally "destroy" terrorist organizations.[11] The first two objectives correctly highlight the primacy of intelligence gathering. Unfortunately, they also presume a clearly defined, static al-Qaeda. The strategy document refers to "command and control and support infrastructure" similar to those of a conventional force that exist at some specific place that can be located. To some extent such infrastructure existed in 2001 when al-Qaeda had a headquarters in Afghanistan. The American invasion of that country forced the terrorists to adopt a more decentralized structure that has neither a nerve center nor even clear regional nodes that can be targeted. This decentralization renders the feasibility of the third objective problematic and the value of achieving it highly questionable. No one seems to know for certain just how many organizations belong to al-Qaeda. Some consist of very few members, others form for the purpose of a single operation, and new ones seem to sprout up as fast as old ones disappear.

The second "D" focuses on ending support for terrorism and includes five objectives. The United States and its allies must "end the state sponsorship of terrorism," "establish and maintain an international standard of accountability with regard to combating terrorism," "strengthen and sustain the international effort to fight terrorism," "interdict and disrupt support for terrorism," and "eliminate terrorist sanctuaries."[12] To accomplish these objectives, the United States and its allies will enable weak states to fight terrorism, persuade reluctant states to join the struggle, and compel unwilling states to stop supporting terrorism.[13] This goal presumes state sponsorship and support of terrorism to be serious problems despite little evidence to support this conclusion. Removal of the Taliban regime and Libya's decision to normalize relations with the West neutralized the only two states known to have directly sponsored terrorist organizations. Although Iran still supports Hezbollah and probably some of the insurgent groups in Iraq, military action to interdict this support would be ill advised even if it were possible. Saudi Arabia does not support al-Qaeda, but some wealthy Saudis do. The state has the unique distinction of being both America's closest ally in the Arab world and a major supporter of terrorism. The vast, complicated network of those who aid and abet terrorist organizations cannot be reduced to traditional concepts of "sponsorship" and "support." Few states that have "terrorist sanctuaries" within their borders condone them; they simply lack the resources to maintain complete sovereignty over the entire national territory.

The third "D" seeks to "diminish the underlying conditions that terrorists seek to exploit" via two objectives: partnering with weak states to strengthen them against the return of terrorism and winning "the war of ideas."[14] Ironically, this most important of the four goals defined by the *National Strategy*, attacking root causes, receives the least attention. The document does not seriously discuss how U.S. foreign policy might address the root causes of terrorism let alone consider that some American actions might actually be making things worse. Nor does it present a reasonable plan for winning the war of ideas, laudable as that goal may be. In fact, misunderstanding and oversimplifying of the ideological basis of al-Qaeda seriously hampers responding to the terrorist threat.

The fourth "D" aims to "defend US citizens and interests at home and abroad." Objectives under this goal include obtaining domain awareness, protecting critical infrastructure, protecting U.S. citizens abroad, and implementing an integrated incident management system.[15] The details of how to implement the fourth "D" may be found in the *National Strategy for Homeland Security*, which defines a range of missions with specific objectives focused primarily on anti-terrorism, consequence management, and intelligence discussed in the previous chapter.[16] This strategy also identifies domestic law enforcement, a *counterterrorism* task, as part of Homeland Security, most of which entails antiterrorism measures.

Assessing the National Strategy

Both the concept and implementation of the *National Strategy for Combatting Terrorism* have been subjects of intense criticism. Jeffrey Record of the Strategic Studies Institute of the U.S. Army War College has described the *National Strategy* as far too simplistic. In particular he challenges its portrayal of terrorism as monolithic and questions the wisdom of making enemies of groups like the Tamil Tigers, who have no intention of attacking the United States, in a war against all terrorists. Record further notes that some groups labeled "terrorist" engage in legitimate resistance to oppressive regimes, no matter how reprehensible the groups' methods may be. Finally, he points out that the *National Strategy* does not consider the prevalent, destructive, and destabilizing effects of terrorism perpetrated by states in today's world.[17]

Another security analyst finds fault with what he describes as the American "grand strategy" after 9/11. He sees the United States arriving at a crossroad where it must weigh short-term benefits against long-term gains. Stephen Biddle argues that in fighting terrorism we must choose between the Cold-War options of containment and rollback. Rolling back terrorism will be a slow methodical, ideological struggle lasting years and with no guarantee of success. Containment, on the other hand, offers a more pragmatic approach to achieving the more reasonable goal of reducing the terrorist threat to an acceptable level. A containment strategy would, for example, place a higher priority on encouraging stability rather than promoting democracy in turbulent regions such as the Middle East.[18] "Operation Rollback," a campaign to support rebellion against Soviet occupation in Eastern Europe, got a lot of people killed but accomplished nothing.[19] Containment, on the other hand, won the Cold War.

In addition to problems noted by these two analysts, the *National Strategy* proceeds from an outdated vision of al-Qaeda. The terrorists no longer organize themselves in the neat hierarchical pyramid the document presents with discrete command-and-control, operational, and support elements that can be easily targeted. They have become a highly decentralized network and a broad-based ideological movement. The *National Strategy* has the United States fighting the al-Qaeda of 2000 not the al-Qaeda of today. This misperception of the enemy has distorted the approach to combating it. Too much emphasis has been placed on attacking states that allegedly sponsor terrorism. The connection between Afghanistan's Taliban regime and al-Qaeda was so demonstrably clear that the United States had no trouble making a compelling case to the American public and the international community for a war to remove it. However, no compelling evidence ever linked Saddam Hussein to al-Qaeda. Osama bin Laden in fact identified the Iraqi regime as an apostate government that should be removed along with those of Saudi Arabia and Egypt. The argument that Saddam possessed nuclear, chemical, and biological weapons that threatened the United States has not been validated, and serious questions about the intelligence used to support this allegation have been raised. Failure to make a compelling case for invading Iraq explains NATO's unwillingness to back "Operation Iraqi Freedom" as it had the invasion of Afghanistan. The Iraq war has seriously damaged relations with many European allies. Far from improving the international security situation, the invasion may actually have made it worse. The power vacuum in Iraq has drawn in *mujahedeen* from all over the Muslim world, much as the Afghan war against the Soviets did in the 1980s. Like their predecessors these foreign fighters may foment terrorism in their own countries when they return home, applying valuable lessons learned on the streets of Baghdad. Iraq has provided both an excellent cause around which to rally support for the al-Qaeda movement and a training ground for a new generation of its operatives.

The Counterinsurgency Model

In a 2003 book I argued that it would be better to think of the struggle with al-Qaeda and its affiliates as a "counterinsurgency campaign on a global scale" rather than as a Global War on Terrorism.[20] The events of the last few years have only strengthened this conclusion. I do not suggest that al-Qaeda should be seen as merely another insurgent organization or that counterinsurgency tactics from past campaigns can be applied as a blueprint for defeating the terrorists. I argue instead for the application of broad counterinsurgency principles to guide a comprehensive response to terrorism (counterterrorism, antiterrorism, consequence management).

As discussed in Chapter 1, insurgency is an effort to gain control of a state from within through a combination of subversion (use of propaganda to persuade others to join or at least support the cause), guerrilla warfare (mounted against troops, police, and government officials), and the limited use of terror for psychological effect. As previously discussed, European nations faced a host of insurgencies against colonial rule during what came to be called "the counterinsurgency era" from 1945 to perhaps 1970.[21] Of those nations only the British enjoyed much success in counterinsurgency. From 1919 to 1960, they developed an effective approach that they applied during the Malayan Emergency, successfully adapted during the Dhofar campaign in Oman, and modified and employed in Northern Ireland.[22] The British approach rested on four broad principles:

1. political and/or economic reform to "win the hearts and minds" of people;
2. closer cooperation between the civil government, the police, and the military;
3. the selective use of force to attack the insurgents without causing unnecessary casualties and alienating people in the process;
4. decentralization of command and control of operations allowing police, military, and civilians considerable latitude in combating insurgents within their local area of authority.[23]

Ideally, the hearts-and-minds campaign would convince people to throw in their lot with the government and provide the security forces the vital intelligence necessary for them to use force in a selective manner. Civil-military cooperation, often formalized through systems of committees, ensured unity of effort while decentralization allowed those with local knowledge to use it in combating the insurgents.

A global campaign of terror perpetrated by a vast decentralized network, of course, differs significantly from an insurgency focused in a single country or region. Studying the details of past counterinsurgency (COIN) campaigns for specific tactics applicable to countering the contemporary terrorist threat would be an exercise in futility. However, the four COIN principles combined in an effective strategy might produce better results than the current GWOT.

Winning Hearts and Minds

To defeat an insurgency a state must understand its causes. People do not rebel without a reason. Insurgency happens because significant elements of a population become disaffected with the existing government for a variety of economic, social, or political reasons. COIN requires a threatened government to examine and address the causes of unrest in order to dissuade more people from joining the insurgents and to win back those who have already defected.

Al-Qaeda terrorism too has root causes in popular disaffection based on at least some legitimate grievances. While few Muslims condone and even fewer support his use of violence, many sympathize with at least some of the goals articulated by bin Laden and his supporters. The United States should consider to what degree American actions might actually be contributing to the unhappiness that motivates terrorists. While neither the West in general nor the United States in particular can be blamed for all the problems in the Muslim World, both have made mistakes and could take steps to correct them.

Foreign policy, like medicine, should be guided by the ancient principle, "at the very least, do no harm." Al-Qaeda only targeted the United States when the American footprint in the Middle East became extremely large during the Gulf War (1991). While it would be hard to question the need to drive Saddam Hussein out of Kuwait, the decision to maintain such a large presence in the region afterwards has to be questioned. U.S. Central Command, which includes the Horn of Africa, the Middle East, and large areas of Central Asia, has replaced European Command as the main theater of military operations. This strategic focus might be maintained without forward deploying so many American service men and women in such a sensitive area. The Iraq War has, unfortunately, put any consideration of a draw-down on hold, but when it ends, the United States might consider moving CENTCOM forces into Southeastern Europe, where many new NATO states would be happy to have them and the economic benefits their presence would bring. The damage caused by recent intervention in the Middle East cannot easily be remedied in the short run, but it should serve as a warning against hasty intervention in other Muslim states.

Beyond avoiding harm some positive foreign policy initiatives might further improve the international security situation. A reevaluation of U. S. policy in the Middle East tops the list of measures to address the root causes of terrorism. To shore up the 1978 Camp David Accords between Israel and Egypt, the United States moved these states to the number one and two spots, respectively, of foreign aide recipients, where they have remained until Iraq temporarily surpassed them both following the U.S. invasion in 2003.[24] For fiscal year 2005 Israel received $2.58 billion and Egypt $1.84 billion in direct aide alone.[25] Military and other assistance programs raised the totals even higher. Most of this money has come with few if any strings attached, freeing Egyptian President Hosni Mubarak from the need to be more accountable to his own people and making it easier for Israel to function without resolving the Palestinian conflict. U.S. policy toward both countries has made it the target of much popular anger that creates sympathy for the terrorists. Ramsi Yousef and the Blind Sheik perpetrated the 1993 World Trade Center bombing because they saw their efforts at Islamist reform in Egypt thwarted by U.S. aide to Mubarak. Anger at U.S. support for Israel fuels much Arab rage that has been exploited by al-Qaeda.

Anger at the United States rose even higher following the Israeli invasion of Lebanon in July 2006. A complex series of events beginning in Gaza led Hezbollah fighters to cross into Israel and attack a military outpost, capturing two Israeli soldiers and killing several others in support of their ally Hamas. This indisputable act of aggression provoked an ill-considered, poorly planned operation that escalated from air strikes to a ground invasion to remove Hezbollah launchers that began to barrage northern Israel with rockets as soon as the first Israeli bombs fell on Lebanon. Without disputing Israel's right of self-defense, many states in the region and in the larger international community questioned the proportionality of the Israeli response. The government of Lebanon, which had little power to control Hezbollah, protested bitterly that Israel had attacked the entire nation, killing many innocent civilians in response to a relatively minor border incident. Although the complex crisis could not be understood, let alone resolved, by assigning blame entirely to one side, the United States did precisely that. Rather than serve as an honest broker, call for a ceasefire, and seek a diplomatic solution, the Bush administration gave Israel its unequivocal support, and proclaimed the conflict another battle in the GWOT. This one-sided approach combined with the daily sight of Israel's American-made F-16s bombing the Lebanese added to anti-American feeling in the Middle East.

The United States need not abandon its two historic allies to improve its image in the Arab and Muslim worlds, but it might hold them more accountable. Aide to Egypt should be made contingent upon democratic reform and aide to Israel dependent upon progress toward peace with the Palestinians. In the case of Egypt, such a move might result in an Islamist government being chosen in truly democratic elections. Such a government might not be a secular Western democracy, but it would not be a Taliban regime either. Washington's willingness to allow such a development could send a strong signal to moderates within the Islamist movement. The United States should continue to support and might even wish to guarantee Israeli security behind the 1967 Green Line, but it should also demand that Israel stop expanding settlements in the occupied territories as a prelude to withdrawing them entirely. The United States, Europe, and the Israeli government might wish to reconsider the policy of refusing to fund or even recognize the new Hamas leadership of the Palestinian authority. Hamas did not recognize Israel nor renounce violence, but it did declare a ceasefire, which ended only after months of Israeli intransigence, economic hardship caused by the cut off of funds, and Israeli strikes that killed a Hamas leader and several civilians. The fighting in Gaza and Lebanon, which broke out in July 2006, developed at least in part from Israel's failure to recognize the Hamas government elected in January of that year. Solving the Israel-Palestine conflict will not, of course, end terrorism, but without achieving a settlement little progress toward reducing popular support for al-Qaeda can be made.

Unforeseen circumstances sometimes create other opportunities to strike a blow against terrorism by improving the image of Americans abroad. The U.S. government, private charities, churches, and individuals made such a contribution to peace following the 2004 tsunami. Congress voted $350 million in humanitarian assistance and $631 million for reconstruction; $400 million of this aide went to Indonesia alone.[26] According to the Pew Charitable Trust's Global Attitudes Survey, the Indonesian perceptions of Americans improved dramatically after the relief effort. Following the reelection of President Bush only 12% of Indonesians had a more favorable feeling toward the United States while 52% had a less favorable feeling. After the Tsunami relief effort 79% had a more favorable feeling, and only 14% had a less favorable one. On the question, "Does US foreign policy consider others' interest?," those who answered, "Yes," rose from 25% in 2003 to 59% in 2005. Indonesia was also one of the few countries in which popular support for the GWOT actually increased, from 23% in 2003 to 50% in 2005.[27] A little charity, it seems, goes a long way. No figures have been gathered for the impact of

U.S. relief to Pakistani earthquake victims, but the Indonesian data suggests the responses would be similar. Good works will not by themselves stop terrorism, but they may weaken popular support for the ideology that drives it.

Another positive step in the foreign policy sphere would be to move away from the strident unilateralism of recent years. Whatever low opinion of the United Nations the American public may hold, many in the rest of the world see it as offering some protection from aggression, especially by the sole remaining superpower. Preemptive military action in the face of imminent threat has always been an option, but past administrations have rarely touted it. Toning down political rhetoric in Washington could have a salutary effect on attitudes toward the United States.

On the domestic front, improving relations with the Muslim community in America might improve relations with the larger Muslim world. The day-to-day treatment of American Muslims belies repeated assurances by politicians that GWOT is not a war on Islam. Muslims (particularly women, whose dress makes them a conspicuous target) have experienced discrimination, racial profiling, and harassment. America's European allies also have an important role to play in the hearts-and-minds campaign. Many of Europe's Muslims live in virtually cloistered communities largely disconnected from the larger societies that view them with at best suspicion and at worst hostility. That the London bombers came from rust belt cities in the north of England surprised no one familiar with Britain's social landscape. Generations of marginalization interspersed with episodes of "Paki bashing" have persuaded many minority youths that they will never be fully accepted as British subjects on a par with their white neighbors. In August 2006 British security forces arrested another group of disaffected young men for plotting to blow up as many as ten airplanes headed for the United States.

A similar pattern of marginalized and embittered Muslim youth acting violently can be found on the Continent. France, where a North African university graduate has only a 1 in 26 chance of landing a decent job in contrast with his white classmate's 1 in 5 opportunity, faces the potential for similar terrorist attacks. This discontent exploded into riots in the fall of 2005, but it could just as easily have resulted in terrorism. If European nations do not find a way to define citizenship in non-ethnic terms, the attacks in London and Madrid and the assassination of Theo Van Gogh in the Netherlands will be harbingers of even worse violence to come.

The Role of the Military and the Limits of Force

The COIN model would make use of military force but to a far more limited degree than the GWOT. Beyond the war in Iraq and the occupation of Afghanistan conventional military forces will have a limited role to play in combating terrorism. Special Forces units will be called upon to turn intelligence leads into productive counterterrorist strikes, but the primary contribution of the armed forces should be in support of nonmilitary responses to terrorism. All three branches of the Armed Services have extensive intelligence and surveillance capabilities, a growing number of language specialists, and considerable technological capacity. These assets can contribute to counterterrorism by supporting law enforcement and covert rather than conventional military operations. The U.S. military will also have a vital role to play in training and educating its counterparts in friendly nations around the world. It can contribute enormously to "hearts-and-minds" operations as the 6th Carrier Battle Group in the Indian Ocean did during the tsunami relief effort.

Conventional military force is a blunt instrument not easily focused on terrorist organizations and networks. The challenge for political leaders will be to resist the temptation to use America's overwhelming military might in ways that will be counterproductive in the long run. The old cliché that "when you are a hammer, everything looks like a nail" especially applies to meeting the terrorist threat. The temptation to find or imagine more state sponsors of terrorism may prove irresistible because the U.S. military is designed to fight other conventional forces. Public pressure to "do something," especially in the aftermath of a devastating attack, can provide an additional incentive to seek a conventional military response to an unconventional threat. Terrorists and insurgents, in fact, deliberately try to provoke a threatened government into overreacting with military force that kills innocent people in the process. The greatest value of the COIN model may be that it emphasizes the primacy of nonmilitary responses to a threat.

Civil-Military Cooperation

The COIN model requires that all responses be incorporated into a comprehensive plan, a grand strategy to deal with the terrorist threat, and a mechanism for coordinating the actions of all those who implement the strategy. In a traditional COIN campaign coordination might be accomplished through a pyramid system of committees as the British set up in Malaya. A global counterterrorism campaign, however, requires a more elaborate integrative structure. Whether such a structure currently exists and more importantly exercises real strategic planning and oversight is a moot point.

In theory the National Security Council could fulfill this role. As the "President's principal forum for considering national security and foreign policy matters with his senior national security advisors and cabinet officials," it has both the mandate and the membership to address

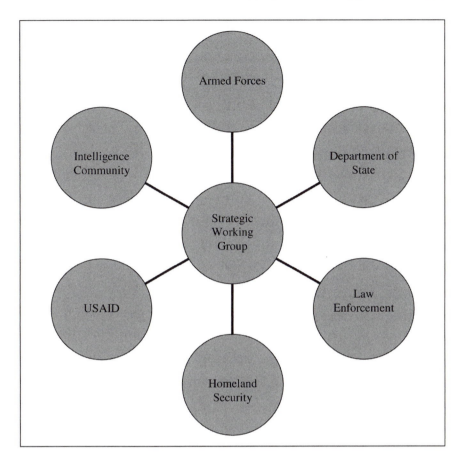

Figure 8.1: Strategic Coordination of Responses to Terrorism.

terrorism.[28] Because it has such broad responsibilities and a policy level focus, however, the National Security Council may not be equipped or prepared to focus intently on a detailed strategy for dealing with terrorism, which despite political rhetoric does not top the list of threats to the United States and its allies. Congress created the Department of Homeland Security (DHS) to deal specifically with lack of coordination between government agencies, but it focuses primarily on antiterrorism and consequence management. The office oversees transportation, customs and borders, immigration, the Secret Service, the Coast Guard, and the Federal Emergency Management Agency (FEMA). It does not control or even coordinate the FBI, CIA, or Department of Defense assets dedicated for responding to terrorism. The Office of the Director of National Intelligence (ODNI) provides another potential mechanism for cooperation, but the ODNI has a mandate limited to intelligence.

No organization, agency, or department has a specific mandate for coordinating responses to terrorism, and it would be inadvisable to create one. A working group devoted exclusively to devising, assessing, and adapting strategy might be advisable and could be housed at the National Counterterrorism Center, which has the facilities and resources to support it. The group would need to be outside the current wire diagram with the ability to report directly to the President. Its membership should be flexible but might begin with representatives from agencies currently charged with various aspects of terrorism response (see Figure 8.1).

Decentralization

Strategic coordination does not, however, mean micromanagement. The decentralized nature of the terrorist threat must be opposed by a sufficiently decentralized and flexible response mechanism. Striking the right balance between strategic oversight and operational decentralization may be difficult. The Department of Homeland Security illustrates this challenge. DHS developed out of a desire to coordinate antiterrorism and consequence management efforts throughout the country by gathering diverse agencies charged with these tasks under one roof. In the long run, the new department may have the desired effect, but it has already shown signs of being overly centralized and top heavy. Placing FEMA within DHS probably decreased its effectiveness in responding to hurricane Katrina, which raises questions about its ability to respond to a terrorist attack.

A similar concern must be raised about the new ODNI. Failure of the FBI and CIA to share information contributed to the 9/11 attacks and revealed the need to facilitate communication between them and among all the intelligence gathering agencies. It remains to be seen, however, whether the ODNI will actually improve intelligence gathering, analysis, and sharing. Too much information flooding into a central bureaucratic organization can overwhelm its ability to analyze that information. The forest disappears into a confusing and ever-increasing array of trees. Intelligence should lead to counterterrorism operations. For that to happen, some analysis must occur at the operational and tactical levels. As British COIN expert Frank Kitson describes the process, the goal is to turn "background information into contact information" in order to create "a chain reaction of analysis alternating with action designed to get information."[29] In other words, good intelligence leads to effective operations which in turn yield more intelligence leading to more operations, etc. This chain reaction usually begins and often ends at the local level. Local intelligence does need to be passed on to a higher body that assembles a comprehensive picture of the terrorists' organization and intentions.

However, if local law enforcement must send information up a chain of command and wait for authorization to act to come back down, the information may be out of date before it can be put to good use. This problem prevented FBI field agents from acting on disturbing intelligence about suspicious individuals taking lessons on how to level-fly commercial airplanes with no interest in learning how to land them. Ideally, the intelligence-operations-intelligence cycle should work like the human reflex mechanism. If a person touches something hot, a reflex arc in his/her spinal cord pulls the hand out of danger while telling the brain (via pain) not to touch the hot object again. If the hand had to wait for the brain to receive the pain message, figure out what to do about the danger, and then send instructions to act, the hand would be badly burned before being drawn away from the hot object.

Maintaining Law and Legitimacy

Winning hearts and minds forms the core of COIN strategy. To deny the insurgents popular support a threatened state must bolster and maintain its own legitimacy. It does so not only by meeting the social, economic, and political needs of its people, but by doing so in a manner that respects the basic rights of its own citizens and even those of captured terrorists. Governments faced with a diffuse threat from an enemy who seems to follow no rules and who kills indiscriminately may be tempted to sink to the same level. In particular, the need to garner effective intelligence in order to catch the terrorists encourages the use of extralegal methods to obtain information. Interrogation (even in normal police investigations) involves making suspects uncomfortable, keeping them off balance, and encouraging them to confess or at least provide information on the crime. At some point, however, pressure becomes abuse and encouragement turns into coercion. The line between interrogation and torture can be easily crossed. No matter what the justification, torture must not become an accepted technique. It seldom yields reliable information, always undermines legitimacy, and damages the counterterrorism campaign in the long run.

The 2004 Abu Ghraib prisoner abuse scandal amply demonstrates the negative impact of torture. Photographs, videos, and eyewitness testimony revealed systematic abuse of inmates at the Iraqi prison. Acting under orders, guards used sleep deprivation, hooding, wall standing (maintaining uncomfortable positions for long periods), intimidation, and humiliating and degrading treatment to "soften up" the detainees for interrogation. The Chinese had used such disorientation techniques on British and American prisoners during the Korean War. The British applied what they had learned from their enemy against insurgents in

Aden (1965–67). When they used them again in Northern Ireland during the internment crisis of the early 1970s, the British government investigated and outlawed practices that amounted to psychological torture. Lord Gardiner, who served on the commission of inquiry investigating interrogation of PIRA suspects, wisely observed that the British should not have abandoned "legal, well-tried and highly successful wartime interrogation methods and replace them by procedures which were secret, illegal, not morally justifiable and alien to the tradition of . . . the greatest democracy in the world."[30] No one at Abu Ghraib seems to have read Gardiner's conclusion. The scandal grew worse when the U.S. military blamed the abuses rather disingenuously on low-ranking personnel who had gotten out of hand. Someone in authority had clearly taught the guards very specific measures to soften up the prisoners.[31]

Since the Abu Ghraib scandal allegations of prisoner abuse at the Guantanamo Bay detention facility have surfaced along with revelations that the United States maintains secret interrogation centers abroad, where it can ignore U.S. law. Some evidence suggests that terrorist suspects have also been turned over to American allies less reluctant to torture them for information. Whether or not these allegations are true, the Iraqi prison scandal makes them much easier for America's critics to believe. It remains very doubtful that torturing these men yielded information of sufficient value to offset the enormous damage to U.S. credibility the scandal has caused.

Maintaining the rule of law does not, however, preclude stern legal measures nor even the temporary suspension of some civil liberties. The British passed emergency legislation granting the authorities extraordinary powers of surveillance and detention without trial during each of their COIN campaigns. They also employed similar measures (Defense of the Realm Acts) within the United Kingdom itself during both World Wars. Abraham Lincoln suspended *habeas corpus* during the American Civil War.

While such draconian measures may be necessary during wartime, they should always be exercised with great caution. The U.S. government has occasionally sanctioned egregious violations of civil liberties and even basic human rights even though they did not contribute to national security. The imprisonment of socialist Eugene V. Debbs for opposing U.S. entry into the First World War and the internment of Japanese Americans as a security measure during World War II provide poignant examples of such abuses. The detention without charge or trial of U.S. citizen Jose Padilla on grounds that he was "an enemy combatant," wiretaps without warrants, and greatly expanded ability of law enforcement to access personal financial, medical, and even library records of ordinary citizens to wage the GWOT have raised valid concerns among civil libertarians. Such abuses of power strengthen the case against calling the struggle with al-

Qaeda a war. Although it may be necessary to suspend some civil liberties in the interest of national security, human rights must never be abrogated. Antiterrorism legislation that suspends, even temporarily, rights of ordinary citizens should be carefully considered, formally activated, periodically reviewed, and deactivated when the emergency has passed.

Privacy versus Security

The struggle with al-Qaeda has created enormous tension between citizens' right to privacy and law enforcements' need to gather intelligence. The debate over this issue reveals a great deal about how people define freedom. Americans are individuals to a fault, often lacking a sense of civic responsibility and unwilling to make sacrifices or even experience inconvenience for the common good. This deeply ingrained national character has made them resistant to even reasonable security measures. On the other hand, abuses of power by both Democratic and Republican administrations, racial profiling by police, and numerous examples of wrongful convictions have created a healthy resistance to ceding too much authority to the local, state, or federal governments. Any extension of law enforcement powers that compromise civil liberties should be subject to intense scrutiny, ample public debate, and careful political deliberation. Unfortunately, once again fear rather than rational assessment based on good information seems to drive the discussion.

The terrorist threat does require adjustment to existing laws and even some compromising of traditional civil liberties, or at least how those rights have been traditionally understood. Wiretap laws passed during the era of the rotary dial had to be adapted to the age of the Internet and the mobile phone. The Foreign Intelligence Surveillance Act (FISA) of 1978 allows for searches and electronic surveillance of a person suspected of spying for a foreign government even without the suspects knowledge. The USA Patriot Act expanded the scope of FISA jurisdiction to include suspects not employed by a foreign government. The FBI would normally apply to a secret FISA court for the requisite warrant, which in an emergency could be granted after the surveillance had begun, hours or even days later. Even such a broad extension of law enforcement powers can be abused. On December 16, 2005, the *New York Times* reported (against the wishes of the White House, which asked them not to publish the story) that a few months after 9/11 President Bush authorized the National Security Agency (NSA) to eavesdrop electronically on Americans and foreign nationals without warrants. Speaking on condition of anonymity, sources familiar with the program said that the NSA spied on about 500 people at any given time without warrants.[32] The Bush administration has defended the program as necessary to fight terrorism and maintains that it focuses on individuals making suspicious calls abroad. Critics argue that given the ease with which the FISA court grants warrants there can be no excuse for not obtaining them. They also raise the concern that the FBI rather than the NSA (subject to far less oversight) should conduct such surveillance once the court approves it. The administration argument that a state of war necessitates such extraordinary measures raises yet another objection to the GWOT.

Although they have raised an enormous hue and cry, surveillance cameras in certain areas also make sense. There should be no expectation of privacy in a public place. Cameras on street corners and in metro stations extend into the public sphere the common use of store security cameras. As the case of the London bombings illustrates, cameras do not prevent all attacks but they aid investigation and may have some deterrent effect on ordinary crime. Terrorists conduct dry runs of planned attacks that may be caught on film. The British have foiled several terrorist plots, perhaps because cameras allowed them to spot suspicious behavior. Surveillance cameras clearly represent a compromise between freedom and security, and their use (particularly storage and distribution of film footage) must be regulated.

National identify cards could also contribute to security, but they trigger such opposition across the political spectrum that they will probably not be used in the foreseeable future. Such cards issued to citizens and legal residents would contain a biometric chip (but not, as commonly presumed, a tracking device) with information on the card holder. This information would be unique to the individual, making it extremely difficult for anyone stealing the card to use it. The chip could also be encrypted with life-saving medical information that most Americans do not now have on their persons (blood type, allergies, conditions, etc.). As a more secure form of personal identification, the cards might also cut down on identity theft. Privacy advocates would do well to consider how much personal information mortgage brokers and credit card companies routinely gather on unsuspecting citizens. Again, the conditions under which law enforcement officers could demand to see and scan the national identity card as well as who would have access to and control of the information on the card would have to be clearly defined and closely regulated. This security measure would make it far more difficult for a terrorist cell to operate anonymously within the United States.

Ironically, many citizens of former communist countries in Central and Eastern Europe are required to carry national identification cards. These people who cherish their freedom from Soviet domination generally do not object to carrying such an id card. They do, however, take great offense at giving up their fingerprint as a condition of entry into the United States. Americans, who must provide their prints to work at host of jobs ranging from teaching to the military, do not find fingerprinting invasive, but they adamantly oppose requiring a national identify card. The government may be sneaking the card in through the back door by requiring proof of citizenship or legal residency as a condition of obtaining a drivers license, a practice many states have already adopted.

Conclusion

Whatever value it may have had in 2001, the GWOT has become a seriously flawed approach to opposing terrorism. This state of war impedes cooperation between the United States and its allies, places far too much emphasis on conventional military responses, and provides cover for a host of unrelated political activities. The counterinsurgency model, particularly as developed by the British over the last century, commends itself as a better model for addressing the terrorist threat. Although COIN and counterterrorism are not identical, they have a great deal in common. COIN requires a comprehensive strategy to address the economic, social and political causes of terrorist violence. In this strategy winning the hearts and minds of disaffected people improves intelligence gathering, which in turn leads to the more focused use of police and military force against terrorist organizations and networks. COIN requires a means of coordinating all strategic activities to ensure unity of effort but considerable decentralization of command and control of counterterrorism operations. In fighting terrorism a threatened state must uphold the rule of law, although it may need to compromise some civil liberties, at least on a temporary basis. Such compromises should, however, be the subject of careful consideration and informed debate rather than the result of hasty measures passed in a climate of fear following an actual attack.

Conclusion: Measuring the Risk and Counting the Cost

When President Franklin Delano Roosevelt told the American public in 1933 that they "had nothing to fear but fear itself," he could hardly have imagined the post-9/11 world. And yet his advice remains as savvy today as it was over seventy years ago. Fear is a powerful and debilitating emotion that often leads to all kinds of destructive behavior. Frightened people cancel travel plans or drive instead of flying (increasing exponentially their risk of dying). They become suspicious of those around them and even hostile to people of a different religion, ethnicity, or race. "Fear," said the late Catholic theologian Henry Nouwen, "breeds a mentality of scarcity."[1] It causes otherwise generous people to hoard whatever they fear will be in short supply. The anthrax attacks following 9/11 made this danger abundantly clear. Americans had pulled together remarkably after the terrorist attacks, but once rumors spread that the antibiotic Cipro might be in short supply, they rushed to get their share, "just in case," without considering that they might be keeping the medicine from people who needed it more than they did. Even some physicians caved in to pressure form their patients and wrote prescriptions they knew that they should not have written. Terrorists of course understand the tremendous power of fear and use it to their advantage. Unfortunately, so do many others. Security companies and gun manufacturers use the emotion to sell their products, and politicians employ it to get elected or at least to boost their ratings in the opinion polls.

The antidote to fear is information. A better understanding of anthrax, realization that antibiotics may cure but cannot prevent the disease, and recognition that the odds of any individual actually getting sick were infinitesimally small might have made for a saner response. Providing such balanced, objective information has been the goal of this book. I have tried to put contemporary terrorism in historical and global perspective, to look for patterns and trends within the phenomenon, to assess vulnerabilities and risks, and to examine the U.S. response to the threat. This study leads me to some general conclusions.

Terror is a weapon that can be used by a variety of state and non-state actors. It has been around a very long time and will be with for us the foreseeable future. The modern use of terror by revolutionaries began about a century and a half ago. Terrorist organizations and methods have evolved as the terrorists learned from their own mistakes and failures. Terrorist campaigns have come and gone, not in neat waves or phases, but as a product of political and social instability in different times and places. In most cases, terror has been used not for its own sake but as part of a broader strategy to achieve a political or ideological goal. The lethality of individual terrorist incidents has increased over time, but the lethality of overall campaigns has not. Attacks have become more deadly because technology now makes it possible for terrorists to kill more people and because television audiences inundated by violent programming do not shock as easily as they once did. Extreme religious ideology also removes the restraint that politically motivated terrorists exercise. Like everything else in the contemporary world, terror has gone global.

Contrary to popular belief, al-Qaeda is not an isolated group of fanatics with limited support. It began as an organization, evolved into a network, and has become a diffuse ideological movement that spawns terrorist cells around the world. An extremist form of Islamist *Salafism* motivates the terrorists who enjoy considerable support and even wider sympathy in many Muslim countries. While very few support terrorism, many people in the Islamist reform movement understand and even agree with at least some of al-Qaeda's ideological goals. Bin Laden and those who share his views seek to remove "heretical" rulers in countries like Egypt and Saudi Arabia as a prelude to their ultimate goal of reestablishing the Caliphate of the eighth century CE. Al-Qaeda targeted the United States only when the organization became convinced that it could not achieve its goals without forcing the United States out of the Middle East. We have been attacked not because we are the enemy but because we are in the way. Even moderate Islamists, however, oppose the Western secularism and "decadence" that increasingly encroaches on their way of life through the Internet, satellite television, and McDonalds.

The nature of the contemporary terrorist threat should dictate the response to it. A threefold approach requires protecting vulnerabilities (antiterrorism), preparing to mitigate the effects of actual terrorist attacks (consequence management), and conducting offensive operations against the terrorists (counterterrorism). Given the impossibility of protecting all potential targets within a vast, open, and diverse society, antiterrorism must be based on sober risk assessment and cost-benefit analysis. Consequence management should take an "all-hazards" response approach, increasing the ability of emergency responders and institutions to handle natural disasters, accidents, and terrorist incidents. Counterterrorism requires pursuing terrorists and attacking terrorist organizations and networks to wear them down in a long-haul campaign. This task falls primarily to law enforcement, Special Forces, and intelligence agencies.

Conventional military forces have an important but limited role to play in this campaign largely in support of other efforts. Overreliance on force can actually increase support for terrorists. Countering al-Qaeda ideology through a more enlightened foreign policy promises better results than invading any more countries.

Above all, this book argues that terrorism should be put in healthy perspective. Despite our preoccupation with the threat over the past five years, the average American is at no greater risk of dying in a terrorist attack today than he or she was on September 10, 2001. Automobile accidents, alcohol, tobacco, drugs, and stress will kill us long before al-Qaeda even finds us. Other Americans with handguns pose a greater threat than do terrorist cells, foreign or domestic. We live in a vast, diverse country heavily dependent on technology, and with an extensive infrastructure. While we can take reasonable steps to lessen the risk of attacks and manage the consequences when they occur, we will never achieve absolute security. Offensive measures can reduce the extent and capabilities of terrorist organizations but not eliminate them. Risk and vulnerability are the price of living in a free and open society. We can face this unsettling truth and get on with our lives or become hostages to our own fears, just as the terrorists wish.

Notes

Chapter 1

1. *Department of Defense Dictionary of Military and Associated Terms, Joint Publication 1-02* (Washington, DC: DOD, 2002), p. 443.

2. Leslie Palti, "Combating Terrorism While Protecting Human Rights," *UN Chronicle* (online edition), vol. XLI (November 4, 2004), http://www.un.org/Pubs/chronicle/2004/issue4/0404cont.htm.

3. David K. Shipler, *Arab and Jew: Wounded Spirits in a Promised Land* (New York: Penguin, 1987), p. 84.

4. Thomas P. Thornton, "Terror as a Weapon of Political Agitation," in *Internal War: Problems and Approaches*, ed. Harry Eckstein (Westport, CT: Praeger, 1964), pp. 72–3.

5. George Rude, *Revolutionary Europe, 1783–1815* (New York: Harper and Row, 1964), p. 74.

6. "When Deadly Force Bumps into Hearts and Minds," *Economist*, January 1, 2005.

7. Bruce Hoffman, *Inside Terrorism* (New York: Columbia University Press, 1998), p. 88.

8. Ibid., p. 87.

9. The Islamist movement, of which al-Qaeda and its affiliates are a part, will be discussed more fully in Chapter 3.

10. Daniel Byman, *Going to War with the Allies You Have: Allies, Counterinsurgency, and the War on Terrorism* (Carlisle Barracks, PA: Strategic Studies Institute, U.S. Army War College, 2005), p. 6.

11. Cited in Thomas R. Mockaitis, *British Counterinsurgency in the Post-Imperial Era* (Manchester, UK: University of Manchester Press, 1995), p. 147.

12. J. Bowyer Bell, "An Irish War," *Small Wars and Insurgencies* 1, no. 3 (December 1990): 244.

13. For a detailed discussion of conditions that led Irish Nationalists to turn from violent conflict to political participation, see Richard English, *Armed Struggle: The History of the IRA* (New York: Oxford University Press, 2003).

14. Christopher Harmon, *Terrorism Today* (London: Frank Cass, 2000), pp. 96–101.

15. Jeanne K. Giraldo and Harold A. Trinkunas, "The Political Economy of Terrorist Financing and State Responses: A Comparative Perspective," unpublished paper, p. 5.

16. Ibid.

17. Ibid., p. 23.

18. Martin McGuinness, quoted in English, *Armed Struggle*, p. 259.

19. Harmon, *Terrorism Today*, p. 186.

20. Ward Churchill, "Some People Push Back: On the Justice of Roosting Chickens," *Free Republic,* http://www.freerepublic.com/focus/f-news/1333883/posts, first published Sept. 12, 2001. The American Indian Movement asserts emphatically that Churchill does not speak for them and even questions his claim to Native American ethnicity: American Indian movement Grand Governing Council Ministry for Information, http://www.aimovement.org/moipr/churchill05.html.

21. Churchill, "Some People Push Back."

Chapter 2

1. See Robert Gellately, *Backing Hitler: Consent and Coercion in Nazi Germany* (New York: Oxford University Press, 2002) for a detailed discussion of the management of Nazi terror.

2. Details on these earlier practitioners of terror from Hoffman, *Inside Terrorism*, pp. 88–89.

3. Johann Most, "Attack is the Best Form of Defense," from *Freiheit*, September 13, 1884, Anarchy Archives: an Online Resource Center on the History and Theory of Anarchism, http://dwardmac.pitzer.edu/Anarchist_Archives/bright/most/attack.html.

4. Sergei Nechaev, *The Revolutionary Catechism*, 1868, online version: http://www.bellum.nu/literature/nechayev001.html.

5. Vladimir Lenin, "Where to begin?" *Lenin Collected Works*, vol. 5 (Moscow: Foreign Languages Publishing House, 1961), pp. 13–24; Marxist Internet Archive, http://www.marxists.org/archive/lenin/works/1901/may/04.htm.

6. Mao Tse-Tung, "Report of an Investigation into the Peasant Movement in Hunan," March 1927, from *Selected Writings of Mao Tse-tung*, vol. 1 (Beijing: Foreign Languages Press, 1963); Marxist Internet Archive, http://www.marxists.org/reference/archive/mao/selected-works/volume-1/mswv1_2.htm.

7. George C. Herring, *America's Longest War: the United States and Vietnam, 1950–1975*, 2nd ed. (New York: Alfred A. Knopf, 1986) argues that the war could not have been won and should not have been fought.

8. See Alistair Horne, "The French Army and the Algerian War," in *Regular Armies and Insurgency*, ed. Ronald Haycock (London: Rowman and Littlefield, 1979), pp. 69–83; and John Pimlott, "The French Army," in *Armed Forces and Modern Counterinsurgency*, eds. Ian Beckett and John Pimlott (New York: St. Martin's, 1985), pp. 46–76.

9. For a detailed discussion of the conflict see John Cloake, *Templer, Tiger of Malaya* (London: Harap, 1985); Richard Clutterbuck, *Riot and Revolution in Singapore and Malaya, 1945–1963* (London: Faber, 1973); and Anthony Short, *The Communist Insurrection in Malaya, 1948–1960* (New York : Muller, 1975). For a discussion of the evolution of the British approach to counterinsurgency culminating with Malaya, see Thomas R. Mockaitis, *British Counterinsurgency, 1919–1960* (London: Macmillan, 1990).

10. Mockaitis, *British Counterinsurgency, 1919–1960*, pp. 46–50; Donald Barnett and Karari Njama, *Mau Mau from Within: Autobiography and Analysis of Kenya's Peasant Revolt* (New York: Monthly Review Press, 1966), pp. 128–9, 209.

11. Brian Lapping, *End of Empire* (New York: St. Martin's Press, 1985), p. 427. Caroline Elkins, *Imperial Reckoning: the Untold Story of Britain's Gulag in Kenya* (New York: Henry Holt & Co., 2005) sets the death rate much higher, but her method of calculating it has been criticized.

12. David Charters, *The British Army and the Jewish Insurgency in Palestine* (London: Macmillan, 1989), pp. 52–60.

13. Ibid., p. 58.

14. Ibid., p. 59.

15. Details of the two massacres from Charles Smith, *Palestine and the Arab-Israeli Conflict*, 5th ed. (New York: Bedford/St. Martins, 2004), p. 194.

16. J. Bowyer Bell, *The Myth of the Guerrilla: Revolutionary Theory and Malpractice* (New York: Knopf, 1971).

17. Jan Oskar Engene, *Terrorism in Western Europe: Explaining the Trends Since 1980* (North Hampton, MA: Edward Elgar, 2004), p. 133.

18. ETA killed 474 people between 1967 and 1995; ibid., p. 129.

19. Ibid., p. 130.

20. Ibid.

21. Mockaitis, *British Counterinsurgency in the Post-Imperial Era*, pp. 96–132.

22. Jonathan Tonge, *Northern Ireland Conflict and Change* (New York: Pearson/ Longman, 2002), p. 88.

23. See Mockaitis, *British Counterinsurgency, 1919-1960*, pp. 72–95.

24. Sean Kendall Anderson and Stephen Sloan, *Terrorism: Assassins to Zealots* (Lanham, MD: the Scarecrow Press, 2003), pp. 231–5.

25. Ibid., p. 361.

26. Yonah Alexander, *Combating Terrorism: Strategies of Ten Countries* (Ann Arbor, MI: University of Michigan Press, 2002), p. 93.

27. Ibid., pp. 106–10.

28. Anderson and Sloan, *Terrorism*, p. 370.

29. Ibid., pp. 397–8.

30. Ibid., p. 349.

31. Hoffman, *Inside Terrorism*, p. 104.

32. Ibid., pp. 102–3.

33. David Rapoport, "Four Waves of Modern Terrorism," *Attacking Terrorism: Elements of Grand Strategy*, eds. Audrey Kurth Cronin and James M. Ludes (Washington, DC: Georgetown University Press, 2004), p. 61.

34. Ibid.

Chapter 3

1. Audrey Kurth Cronin, "Sources of Contemporary Terrorism," in *Attacking Terrorism*, pp.19–45.

2. Rapoport, "Four Waves of Modern Terrorism," p. 75.

3. Ibid., p. 61.

4. Harmon, *Terrorism Today*.

5. Figures are drawn from MIPT Terrorism Knowledge Base, http://www.tkb.org/Home.jsp; Figures for 1968–98 include only international incidents while those since 1998 include both domestic and international incidents.

6. Ibid.

7. Ibid.

8. Aaron Clauset and Maxwell Young, "Scale Invariance in Global Terrorism," Physics/0502014, March 6, 2006, Cornell University Library e-prints in Physics, Mathematics, Computer Science and Quantitative Biology, http://arxiv.org/PS_cache/physics/pdf/0502/0502014.pdf. The authors do not include the Russian Federation in what is now the G8, but the Moscow theater and Beslan school bombings would seem to support the authors' conclusions.

9. MIPT Terrorism Knowledge Base.

10. Gabriel Weimann, *www.terror.net: How Modern Terrorism Uses the Internet* (Washington, DC: U.S. Institute of Peace, 2004), p. 2 (Online version at http://wwwusip.org/pubs/speicalrceports/sr116.html).

11. Ibid., p. 3

12. Ibid., pp. 4–9.

13. See, for example, the website, *Everything2*, http://everything2.com/index.pl?node_id=1076813.

14. "Terrorist Activities on the Internet," *Terrorism Update* (Winter 1998), Anti-Defamation League web site, http://www.adl.org/terror/focus/16_focus_a.asp.

15. Quoted in "Online Support Grows for Iraq's 'Prince of Cutthroats'," *Taipei Times*, October 6, 2004, online edition, http://www.taipeitimes.com/News/world/archives/2004/10/06/2003205773.

16. Peter Bergen, quoted in Tom Regan, "Terrorism and the 'Net'", *Christian Science Monitor*, October 7, 2004, online edition, http://www.csmonitor.com/2004/1007/dailyUpdate.html?s=rsst.

17. Richard Clutterbuck, *Terrorism and Guerrilla Warfare: Forecasts and Remedies* (New York: Routledge, 1990), p. 129, cited in Alexander, *Combating Terrorism*, p. 101.

18. See Benjamin Barber, *Jihad vs. McWorld* (New York: Times Books/Random House, 1995) and Jamal R. Nassar, *Globalization and Terrorism: The Migration of Dreams and Nightmares* (New York: Rowan and Littlefield, 2005) for a discussion of these issues.

19. Jessica Stern, *Terror in the Name of God: Why Religious Militants Kill* (New York: Harper Collins, 2003), pp. 63–84.

20. Ibid., pp. 85–138. Stern discusses "History" and "Territory" as separate grievances motivating religious terrorism, when in fact they usually operate together.

21. Ibid., pp. 9–31.

22. Ibid., pp. 37–38.

23. Nasra Hassan, "Are You Ready? Tomorrow You Will Be in Paradise . . .," *Times Online*, July 14, 2005, http://www.timesonline.co.uk/article/0,,7-1692606,00.html.

24. As will be seen, suicide bombers who attacked the London underground defied these guidelines.

25. Hassan, "Are You Ready?"

26. Brian Handwerk, "Female Suicide Bombers: Dying to Kill," *National Geographic News online*, December 13, 2004, http://news.nationalgeographic.com/news/2004/12/1213_041213_tv_suicide_bombers.html.

Chapter 4

1. Samuel P. Huntington, "Is there a Clash of Civilizations?" *Foreign Affairs* 7, no. 3 (Summer 1993): 22–28. Quotes from Samuel P. Huntington, *The Clash of Civilizations and the Remaking of World Order* (New York: Simon & Schuster, 1996), pp. 20, 28.

2. Bernard Lewis, *What Went Wrong?: The Clash between Islam and Modernity in the Middle East* (New York: Harper Perennial, 2003).

3. Biographical sketch based on Rohan Gunaratna, *Inside Al Qaeda, Global Network of Terror* (New York: Columbia University Press, 2002), pp. 16–17.

4. Transcript of Osama bin Laden interview with Peter Arnett, CNN, March 1997, http://www.anusha.com/osamaint.htm.

5. Peter L. Bergen, *Holy War, Inc.: Inside the Secret World of Osama bin Laden* (New York: the Free Press, 2001), p. 78; Gunaratna has bin Laden returning first to Pakistan in 1991, *Inside Al Qaeda*, p. 29.

6. Bergen, *Holy War, Inc.*, p. 31.

7. Ibid.

8. Ibid.

9. Jodie Allen, ed., *Islamic Extremism: Common Concern for Muslim and Western Publics* (Washington, DC: Pew Charitable Trust, 2005), p. 6, online version, http://www.pewtrusts.com/pdf/PRC_global_Terror_0705.pdf. Confidence in bin Laden dropped considerably in Indonesia, where it had been 58% in 2003, and Morocco, where it had been 49% in 2003.

10. Gunaratna, *Inside Al Qaeda*, p. 21.

11. Stern, *Terror in the Name of God*, p. 250.

12. Gunaratna, *Inside Al Qaeda*, p. 10.

13. Account based on that given by Stern, *Terror in the Name of God*, pp. 239–45. Stern had access to classified evidence from Mohamed's trial.

14. Bergen, *Holy War, Inc.*, p. 30.

15. Gunaratna, *Inside Al Qaeda*, p. 79.

16. Ibid., p. 13.

17. Ibid., p. 8.

18. Bergen, *Holy War, Inc.*, p. 90.

19. Ibid., p. 85; Stern, *Terror in the Name of God*, p. 253.

20. Gunaratna, *Inside Al Qaeda*, p. 45.

21. Michael Chandler, "The Global Threat from Transnational Terrorism: How it is Evolving and its Impact in Europe," Power Point presentation, The George C. Marshall European Center for Security Studies, July 19–21, 2005.

22. Sebastian Rotella, "Who Guided London's Attackers?" *Los Angeles Times*, March 6, 2006, p. A1.

23. Ibid.

24. "The New Al-Qaeda: jihad.com," BBC News online, July 25, 2005, http://newsvote.bbc.co.uk/go/pr/fr/-/1/programmes/4683403.stm.

25. Ibid.

26. Bergen, *Holy War, Inc.*, p. 27.

27. Memorial Institute for the Prevention of Terrorism (MIPT) Terrorism Knowledge Base.

28. Gunaratna, *Inside Al Qaeda*, p. 6.

29. Bergen, *Holy War, Inc.*, p. 22.

30. MIPT Terrorism Knowledge Base.

31. Ibid.

32. Ibid.

33. Details of the attack from MIPT Terrorism Knowledge Base and BBC News Online, http://news.bbc.co.uk/1/hi/in_depth/uk/2005/london_explosions/default.stm.

34. Ibid., http://news.bbc.co.uk/1/hi/uk/4206708.stm.

35. MIPT Terrorism Knowledge Base.

Chapter 5

1. Gilles Kepel, *Jihad: the Trail of Political Islam*, translated by Anthony F. Roberts (Cambridge, MA: The Belknap Press of Harvard University Press, 2002), pp. 24–27.

2. Ibid., p. 26.

3. Excerpts from *Knights Under the Prophets Banner* (London: Al-Sharq al-Awsat Publishers, 2001), translated by Foreign Broadcast Service, Document Number: FBIS-NES-2002-0108, available from Fundación Burgos por la Investigación de la Salud to subscribers at www.fbis.org.

4. Osama bin Laden, Interview with Peter Arnett.

5. "Mujahid Usamah Bin Laden Talks Exclusively to *Nida'ul Islam* about the New Powder Keg in the Middle East," *Nida'ul Islam*, 15 (October-November 1996), translated and posted on Federation of American Scientists (FAS) web page: http://www.fas.org/irp/world/para/docs/LADIN.htm.

6. Osama bin Laden, Interview with Peter Arnett.

7. Ibid.

8. Bergen, *Holy War, Inc.*, p. 19.

9. "Jihad Against Jews and Crusaders," World Islamic Statement translated, FAS web page, http://www.fas.org/irp/world/para/docs/980223-fatwa.htm.

10. Full transcript of bin Laden's Speech, October 30, 2004, on the Aljazeera Television web page, http://english.aljazeera.net/NR/exeres/554FAF3A-B267-427A-B9EC-54881BDE0A2E.htm?printguid={79C6AF22-98FB-4A1C-B21F-2BC36E87F61F}.

11. Letter from Abu Muhammad al-Zawahiri to Abu Musab al-Zarqawi, July 9, 2005, translated on FAS website, http://www.fas.org/irp/news/2005/10/letter_in_english.pdf. The authenticity of the document is probably less important than what it reveals about the terrorists' motives.

12. Nassar, *Globalization and Terrorism*, pp. 12, 13.

13. "Bin Laden Talks Exclusively to *Nida'ul Islam*."

14. Bergen, *Holy War, Inc.*, p. 26.

15. Text of message from al-Zarqawi, April 6, 2004, translated on FAS website, http://www.fas.org/irp/world/para/zarqawi040604.html.

16. Barber, *Jihad vs. McWorld,,* p. 17.

17. Ibid., p. 155.

18. See Sherifa Zuhur, *A Hundred Osamas: Islamist Threats and the Future of Counterinsurgency* (Carlisle Barracks, PA: Strategic Studies Institute, U.S. Army War College, 2005).

19. MIPT Terrorism Knowledge Base.

20. Ibid.

21. Information on differences between Sunni and Shiite Islam may be found on "Islamic Web", http://islamicweb.com/?folder=beliefs.

22. Ibid.

23. Explanation of Jihad is based on Seyyed Hossein Nasr, Professor of Islamic Studies, George Washington University, "Spiritual Significance of Jihad," http://www.islamicity.com/articles/Articles.asp?ref=IC0407-2391.

24. *Al-Hayat,* Islamic Research Council of al-Azhar University, November 5, 2001, cited in John Esposito, *Unholy War: Terror in the Name of Islam* (New York: Oxford University Press, 2002), p. 158.

25. Zuhur, *A Hundred Osamas,* p. 51.

26. "Is Islamism a Threat? A Debate," *Middle East Quarterly* 6, no. 4 (December 1999), online version, http://www.meforum.org/article/447.

27. Bernard Haykel, "Radical Salafism: Osama's Ideology," 2001, http://muslim-canada.org/binladendawn.html#copyrightauthor. The author teaches Islamic Law at New York University.

28. Kepel, *Jihad,* p. 220.

29. Ibid., p. 51.

30. Ibid., p. 219.

31. Zuhur, *A Hundred Osamas,* pp. 19–21.

32. Ibid.

Chapter 6

1. Geographic details from the *CIA World Fact Book,* March 29, 2006, http://www.cia.gov/cia/publications/factbook/geos/iz.html.

2. Anthony H. Cordesman, *Terrorism, Asymmetric Warfare, and Weapons of Mass Destruction: Defending the U.S. Homeland* (Westport, CT: Praeger, 2002), p. 39.

3. Stephen E. Flynn, "The Unguarded Homeland: A Study in Malign Neglect," in *How Did This Happen: Terrorism and the New War,* eds. James F. Hodges and Gideon Rose (New York: Public Affairs, 2001), p. 183.

4. Allison Tarman, "Number of U.S. Undocumented Migrants Rises, but Policy Response Still Lacking," Population Reference Bureau, http://www.prb.org/Template.cfm?Section=PRB&template=/ContentManagement/ContentDisplay.cfm&ContentID=12344.

5. *CIA World Fact Book.*

6. "What are the Odds of Dying?" National Safety Council, http://www.nsc.org/lrs/statinfo/odds.htm.

7. "What odds are you comfortable with?" National Safety Council, http://www.anotherperspective.org/advoc530.html, accessed August 21, 2006. These numbers are based on Center for Disease Control data.

8. *Special Report of the Special Advisor to the DCI on Iraq's Weapons of Mass Destruction*, (Washington DC: Government Printing Office, 2004), vol. 3, Glossary.

9. Jonathan Medalia, *Nuclear Terrorism: A Brief Review of Threats and Responses* (Washington, DC: Congressional Research Service, 2004), p. 1.

10. Ibid., p. 3.

11. Ibid.

12. Ibid. p. 10.

13. Henry Kelly, "Dirty Bombs, a Response to the Threat," *The Journal of the Federation of American Scientists* 55, no. 2 (March/April 2002), electronic version, http://www.fas.org/faspir/2002/v55n2/dirtybomb.htm.

14. *Chernobyl Forum: 2003-2005, Chernobyl's Legacy: Health, Environmental and Socio-Economic Impacts and Recommendations to the Governments of Belarus, the Russian Federation and Ukraine*, International Atomic Energy Commission, 2nd revised edition, http://www.iaea.org/Publications/Booklets/Chernobyl/chernobyl.pdf.

15. "Spent Fuel Stored in Pools at Some U.S. Nuclear Power Plants Potentially at Risk From Terrorist Attacks; Prompt Measures Needed to Reduce Vulnerabilities," National Academy of Sciences Press Release, April 6, 2005, http://www.nationalacademies.org/news.nsf/isbn/0309096472?OpenDocument.

16. Discussion of chemical agents based on Cordesman, *Terrorism, Asymmetric Warfare, and Weapons of Mass Destruction*, pp. 114–6. The author also considers agents that incapacitate rather than kill.

17. Amy E. Smithson, "Grounding the Threat in Reality," in *Ataxia: The Chemical and Biological Terrorism Threat and the US Response*, Amy E. Smithson and Leslie-Anne Levy (Washington, DC: Henry L. Stimson Center, 2000), pp. 34–35.

18. Ibid., p. 37.

19. Ibid., p. 38.

20. "Bioterrorism Overview," Centers for Disease Control and Prevention, http://www.bt.cdc.gov/bioterrorism/overview.asp.

21. Smithson, "Grounding the Threat in Reality," p. 55.

22. *Questions and Answers about Ebola Hemorrhagic Fever*, Centers for Disease Control and Prevention, http://www.cdc.gov/ncidod/dvrd/spb/mnpages/dispages/ebola/qa.htm.

23. Cordesman, *Terrorism, Asymmetric Warfare, and Weapons of Mass Destruction*, pp. 137–45.

24. *Frequently Asked Questions About Smallpox*, Centers for Disease Control and Prevention, http://www.bt.cdc.gov/agent/smallpox/disease/faq.asp.

25. Chris L. Barrett, Stephen G. Eubank, and James P. Smith, "If Smallpox Strikes Portland . . .," *Scientific American* (March 2005), pp. 54–61.

26. *Bacillus Anthracis*, Centers for Disease Control and Prevention briefing, Oct. 31, 2001, http://www.bt.cdc.gov/agent/anthrax/SlideSetAnthrax.pdf.

27. *Adherence to and Compliance with Arms Control and Nonproliferation Agreements and Commitments* (Washington, DC: Bureau of Compliance, 2001), http://www.state.gov/t/vci/rls/rpt/22322.htm.

28. Milton Leitenberg, *Assessing the Biological Weapons and Bioterrorism Threat* (Carlisle Barracks, PA: U.S. Army War College, Strategic Studies Institute, 2005), p. 14.

29. Ibid., pp. 28–42.

30. Nadine Gurr and Benjamin Cole, *The Face of Terrorism: Threats from Weapons of Mass Destruction* (New York: I.B. Tauris, 2000), p. 64. The authors suggest that cruder forms of aeresolization could be used but do not provide details. They also speculate that terrorists might overcome the problem in the future, but again do not specify how.

31. Details on distribution difficulties form Smithson, "Grounding the Threat in Reality," pp. 53–54.

32. Gary Ackerman and Cheryl Loeb, "Much Ado Over Anthrax," *San Diego Tribune*, October 21, 2001, http://cns.miis.edu/pubs/other/muchado.htm.

33. Cordesman, *Terrorism, Asymmetric Warfare, and Weapons of Mass Destruction*, pp. 137–45.

Chapter 7

1. *NATO's Military Concept for Defense Against Terrorism*, November 21, 2002, NATO International Military Staff, http://www.nato.int/ims/docu/terrorism.htm.

2. "Undertakings of the Department of Homeland Security, Bureau of Customs, and Border Protection," May 11, 2004, U.S. Department of Homeland Security, http://www.dhs.gov/interweb/assetlibrary/CBP-DHS_PNRUndertakings5-25-04.pdf.

3. "TSA Begins Third Phase of Rail Security Experiment," Transportation Safety Administration Press Release, July 15, 2004.

4. Steve Dunham, "Mass Transit Defends Itself," *Journal of Homeland Security*, March 2002, http://www.homelandsecurity.org/newjournal/articles/dunhammasstransit.htm.

5. *National Strategy for Maritime Security* (Washington, DC: Department of Homeland Security, 2005), p. 1.

6. Cordesman, *Terrorism, Asymmetric Warfare and Weapons of Mass Destruction*, p. 39.

7. *National Strategy for Maritime Security*, p. 4.

8. Ibid.

9. "Fact Sheet, Securing U.S. Ports," Department of Homeland Security Press Release, http://www.dhs.gov/dhspublic/interapp/press_release/press_release_0865.xml

10. Ibid.

11. *National Strategy for Maritime Security*, p. 17.

12. "Threats and Protection," Department of Homeland Security, http://www.dhs.gov/dhspublic/theme_home6.jsp.

13. London Assembly, *Report of the 7 July Review Committee* (London: Greater London Authority, 2006), pp. 123–41.

14. See Rod Propst, "Enhancing Disaster Management through an All-Hazards Continuity-of-Operations Continuum," *Journal of Homeland Security* (March 2006) for a discussion of this process.

15. *National Response Plan* (Washington, DC: Department of Homeland Security, 2004), p. iii. "Tribal" refers to Native American.

16. "Fact Sheet: Plots, Casings, and Infiltrations Referenced in President Bush's Remarks on the War on Terror," The White House, October 2005, http://www.whitehouse.gov/news/releases/2005/10/20051006-7.html.

17. "Protecting America Against Terrorist Attack, A Closer Look at the FBI's Joint Terrorism Task Forces," Federal Bureau of Investigation, December 1, 2004, http://www.fbi.gov/page2/dec04/jttf120114.htm.

18. Terrorist Screening Center, Mission Statement, Federal Bureau of Investigation, http://www.fbi.gov/terrorinfo/counterterrorism/mission.htm.

19. Statement of John S. Pistole, Executive Assistant Director, Counterterrorism/Counterintelligence, FBI, Before the National Commission on Terrorist Attacks upon the United States, April 14, 2004, http://www.fbi.gov/congress/congress04/pistole041404.htm.

20. Summary of USA Patriotic Act, H.R. 3162, October 24, 2001, Library of Congress, http://thomas.loc.gov/cgi-bin/bdquery/z?d107:HR03162:@@@D&summ2=m&.

21. Giraldo and Trinkunus, "Political Economy of Terrorist Financing," p. 25.

22. Figures for 9/11 and Madrid from Giraldo and Trinkunus, "Political Economy of Terrorist Financing," p.23. The figure for the London bombings is from Tariq Panja, "Analysts Say London Bombings Inexpensive," ABC News International, January 3, 2006, http://www.abcnews.go.com/International/Terrorism/wireStory?id=1466463.

23. Phil Williams, "Warning Indicators and Terrorist Financing," in Giraldo and Trinkunas, "Political Economy of Terrorist Financing," pp. 18–20.

24. Frank Kitson, *Low-Intensity Operations* (London: Faber and Faber, 1971), p. 65.

25. *The 9/11 Commission Report* (Washington, DC: Government Printing Office, 2004), p. 400.

26. Office of the Director of Intelligence Mission Statement, http://www.dni.gov/aboutODNI/mission.htm.

27. "About the National Counterterrorism Center," National Counterterrorism Center, http://www.nctc.gov/about_us/about_nctc.html.

28. NCTC Task List, National Counterterrorism Center, http://www.nctc.gov/about_us/how_we_do.html.

29. Richard Posner, "The 9/11 Report: a Dissent," *The New York Times Book Review*, August 29, 2004, Section 7, Column 1, p. 1.

30. "Brief NIC History," National Intelligence Council, http://www.dni.gov/nic/NIC_history.html.

31. James Risen, *State of War: the Secret History of the CIA and the Bush Administration* (New York: Free Press, 2006).

Chapter 8

1. Representative Brad Sherman, "America Must Wage War Against Terrorism," 107th Cong., 1st sess., *Congressional Record* (September 11, 2001).

2. *Authorizing use of United States Armed Forces against those responsible for recent attacks against the United States*, H.J. Res. 64, 107th Cong., 1st sess., *Congressional Record* (September 14, 2001). The House made clear that they were not formally declaring war.

3. "Address to the Nation by the President of the United States," September 20, 2001, *Congressional Record* (September 20, 2001): H5859–H5862.

4. "NATO's Response to Terrorism," Statement issued at North Atlantic Council Ministers Meeting, Brussels, December 6, 2001, NATO Ministerials, http://www.nato.int/docu/pr/2001/p01-159e.htm.

5. UN Security Council Resolution 1368 (2001), UN document S/RES/1368 (2001), adopted September 12, 2001.

6. "No Nation Can Be Neutral in This Conflict," Remarks by President Bush to the Warsaw Conference on Combating Terrorism, November 6, 2001, The White House, http://www.whitehouse.gov/news/releases/2001/11/20011106-2.html.

7. *National Strategy for Combating Terrorism* (Washington, DC: Government Printing Office, 2003), p. 12.

8. President's address to the Nation, September 20, 2001.

9. Ibid., p. 1.

10. Ibid., p. 15.

11. Ibid., p. 16.

12. Ibid., p. 17–22.

13. Ibid., pp. 20–21.

14. Ibid., pp. 23–24.

15. Ibid., pp. 24–28.

16. *National Strategy for Homeland Security* (Washington, DC: Government Printing Office, 2002).

17. Jeffrey Record, *Bounding the Global War on Terrorism* (Carlisle Barracks, PA: Strategic Studies Institute, December 2003).

18. Stephen Biddle, *American Grand Strategy after 9/11* (Carlisle Barracks, PA: Strategic Studies Institute, April 2005).

19. See Peter Grose, *Operation Rollback: America's Secret War behind the Iron Curtain* (New York: Houghton Mifflin, 2000) for a discussion of this operation.

20. Thomas R. Mockaitis, "Winning Hearts and Minds in the 'War on Terrorism'," in *Grand Strategy in the War on Terrorism*, eds. Thomas R. Mockaitis and Paul Rich (London: Frank Cass, 2003), p. 21. In his testimony before Congress two years later, Rand Corporation terrorism expert Bruce Hoffman made precisely the same argument that it would be more useful to reconceptualize GWOT as GCOIN (global counterinsurgency). Bruce Hoffman, *Does Our Counter-Terrorism Strategy Match the Threat?*, Testimony before the House Foreign Relations Committee, Sept. 29, 2005 (Santa Monica, CA: Rand, 2005), p. 11.

21. Douglas Blaufarb, *The Counterinsurgency Era: US Doctrine and Performance, 1950 to the Present* (New York: Free Press, 1977).

22. See Mockaitis, *British Counterinsurgency, 1919-1960* and *British Counterinsurgency in the Post-imperial Era*, for a discussion of the evolution of the British

approach. Britain did suffered defeat by insurgents in Palestine (1945-47) and South Arabia (1964-67).

23. Mockaitis, *British Counterinsurgency, 1919-1960* and *British Counterinsurgency in the Post-imperial Era.*

24. Curt Tarnoff and Larry Nowels, *Foreign Aid: An Introductory Overview of US Programs and Policy* (Washington: Congressional Research Service, 2004), p. 13. The two countries now hold the second and third spots.

25. Curt Tarnoff and Larry Nowels, *Foreign Aid: An Introductory Overview of US Programs and Policy* (Washington: Congressional Research Service, 2005), p. 14.

26. "USAID Rebuilds Lives After the Tsunami," Update, April 27, 2006, U.S. Agency for International Development, http://www.usaid.gov/locations/asia_near_east/tsunami/index.html.

27. *The Pew Global Attitudes Project* (Washington, DC: Pew Charitable Trust, 2005), pp. 3–4, 28.

28. "National Security Council's Function," National Security Council, http://www.whitehouse.gov/nsc/.

29. Frank Kitson, *Bunch of Five* (London: Faber and Faber, 1977), pp. 296, 298.

30. Lord Gardiner, *Minority Report of the Commission Appointed to Consider Procedures for Interrogating Prisoners Suspected of Terrorism* (Parker Commission), Cmd. 4901 (London: HMSO, 1972). The prime minister accepted the minority report.

31. Thomas R. Mockaitis, "Unlearned Lessons From a Forgotten War," *Chicago Tribune*, May 14, 2004, p. 29.

32. James Risen and Eric Lichtblau, "Bush Lets U.S. Spy on Callers without Courts," *New York Times*, Dec. 16, 2005, p. A 1. Risen expanded on the article in *State of War.*

Conclusion

1. Henry Nouwen (public address, River Grove, IL, 1983).

Bibliography

U.S. Government Documents

Library of Congress, Summary of USA Patriotic Act. http://thomas.loc.gov/cgi-bin/bdquery/z?d107:HR03162:@@@D&summ2=m&.

Medalia, Jonathan. *Nuclear Terrorism: A Brief Review of Threats and Responses*. Washington, DC: Congressional Research Service, 2004.

National Strategy for Combating Terrorism. Washington, DC: Government Printing Office, 2003.

National Strategy for Homeland Security. Washington, DC: Government Printing Office, 2002.

9/11 Commission. *The 9/11 Commission Report*. Washington, DC: Government Printing Office, 2004.

U.S. Congress. *Congressional Record*. 107th Congress, 1st sess., 2001.

U.S. Department of Defense. *Department of Defense Dictionary of Military and Associated Terms, Joint Publication 1-02*. Washington, DC: Department of Defense, 2002.

U.S. Department of Homeland Security. *National Response Plan*. Washington, DC: Government Printing Office, 2004.

———. *National Strategy for Maritime Security*. Washington, DC: Government Printing Office, 2005, p. 1, http://www.dhs.gov/interweb/assetlibrary/HSPD13_MaritimeSecurityStrategy.pdf.

U.S. Department of State. *Adherence to and Compliance with Arms Control and Nonproliferation Agreements and Commitments*. Washington, DC: Bureau of Compliance, 2001.

U.S. Transportation and Safety Administration. "TSA Begins Third Phase of Rail Security Experiment," TSA Press Release, July 15, 2004.

NATO Document

NATO's Military Concept for Defense Against Terrorism, 21 Nov. 2002, http://www.nato.int/ims/docu/terrorism.htm.

Reports by Non-governmental Organizations

International Atomic Energy Commission. *Chernobyl Forum: 2003-2005, Chernobyl's Legacy: Health, Environmental and Socio-Economic Impacts and Recommendations to the Governments of Belarus, the Russian Federation and Ukraine*. Vienna: International Atomic Energy Agency, 2006. 2nd revised edition.

Also available at http://www.iaea.org/Publications/Booklets/Chernobyl/chernobyl.pdf.

National Academy of Sciences. "Spent Fuel Stored in Pools at Some U.S. Nuclear Power Plants Potentially at Risk From Terrorist Attacks; Prompt Measures Needed to Reduce Vulnerabilities." National Academy of Sciences press release, April 6, 2005. http://www4.nationalacademies.org/news.nsf/isbn/0309096472?OpenDocument (accessed May 2006).

Pew Research Center. *Islamic Extremism: Common Concern for Muslim and Western Publics.* Edited by Jodie Allen. Washington, DC: Pew Charitable Trust, 2005. Online version at http://www.pewtrusts.com/pdf/PRC_global_Terror_0705.pdf.

Smithson, Amy E. "Grounding the Threat in Reality." In *Ataxia: The Chemical and Biological Terrorism Threat and the US Response.* Amy E. Smithson and Leslie-Anne Levy. Washington, DC: Henry L. Stimson Center, 2000.

Tarman, Allison. "Number of U.S. Undocumented Migrants Rises, but Policy Response Still Lacking." Population Reference Bureau. http://www.prb.org/Template.cfm?Section=PRB&template=/ContentManagement/ContentDisplay.cfm&ContentID=12344.

Al-Qaeda Statements and Publications

al-Zarqawi, Abu Musab. Text of message from April 6, 2004. Translated on Federation of American Scientists (FAS) website, http://www.fas.org/irp/world/para/zarqawi040604.html.

al-Zawahiri, Ayman. Letter from Ayman al-Zawahiri to Abu Musab al-Zarqawi, July 9, 2005. Translated on FAS website. http://www.fas.org/irp/news/2005/10/letter_in_english.pdf.

———. *Knights Under the Prophet's Banner.* London: London Al-Sharq al-Awsat Publishers, 2001. Translated by Foreign Broadcast Service, Document Number: FBIS-NES-2002-0108, www.fbis.org.

bin Laden, Osama. Full transcript of speech, October 30, 2004, Aljazeera, http://english.aljazeera.net/NR/exeres/554FAF3A-B267-427A-B9EC-54881BDE0A2E.htm?printguid={79C6AF22-98FB-4A1C-B21F-2BC36E87F61F}

———. "Mujahid Usamah Bin Laden Talks Exclusively to *Nida'ul Islam* about the New Powder Keg in the Middle East." *Nida'ul Islam,* 15 (October-November 1996). Translated and posted on FAS web page: http://www.fas.org/irp/world/para/docs/LADIN.htm.

———. Transcript of interview with Peter Arnett, CNN, March 1997. http://www.anusha.com/osamaint.htm.

"Jihad Against Jews and Crusaders." World Islamic Statement February 23, 1998. Translation found on FAS web page, www.fas.org/irp/world/para/docs/980223-fatwa.htm.

Books

Alexander, Yonah. *Combating Terrorism: Strategies of Ten Countries.* Ann Arbor, MI: University of Michigan Press, 2002.

Anderson, Sean Kendall, and Stephen Sloan. *Terrorism: Assassins to Zealots.* Lanham, MD: Scarecrow Press, 2003.

Barber, Benjamin. *Jihad vs. McWorld.* New York: Times Books/Random House, 1995.

Barnett, Donald, and Karari Njama, *Mau Mau from Within: Autobiography and Analysis of Kenya's Peasant Revolt.* New York: Monthly Review Press, 1966.

Bergen, Peter L. *Holy War, Inc.: Inside the Secret World of Osama bin Laden.* New York: Free Press, 2001.

Bowyer Bell, J. *Myth of the Guerrilla: Revolutionary Theory and Malpractice.* New York: Knopf, 1971.

Charters, David. *The British Army and the Jewish Insurgency in Palestine.* London: Macmillan, 1989.

Cloake, John. *Templer, Tiger of Malaya.* London: Harap, 1985.

Clutterbuck, Richard. *Riot and Revolution in Singapore and Malaya, 1945-1963.* London: Faber, 1973.

———. *Terrorism and Guerrilla Warfare: Forecasts and Remedies.* New York: Routledge, 1990.

Cordesman, Anthony H. *Terrorism, Asymmetric Warfare, and Weapons of Mass Destruction: Defending the U.S. Homeland.* Westport, CT: Praeger, 2002.

Cronin, Audrey Kurth. "Sources of Contemporary Terrorism." *Attacking Terrorism: Elements of Grand Strategy.* Edited by Audrey Kurth Cronin and James M. Ludes. Washington, DC: Georgetown University Press, 2004.

Engene, Jan Oskar. *Terrorism in Western Europe: Explaining the Trends since 1980.* North Hampton, MA: Edward Elgar, 2004.

English, Richard. *Armed Struggle: the History of the IRA.* New York: Oxford University Press, 2005.

Esposito, John. *Unholy War: Terror in the Name of Islam.* New York: Oxford University Press, 2002.

Gellately, Robert. *Backing Hitler: Consent and Coercion in Nazi Germany.* New York: Oxford University Press, 2002.

Gunaratna, Rohan. *Inside Al Qaeda, Global Network of Terror.* New York: Columbia University Press, 2002.

Gurr, Nadine, and Benjamin Cole, *The Face of Terrorism: Threats from Weapons of Mass Destruction.* New York: I.B. Tauris, 2000.

Harmon, Christopher. *Terrorism Today.* London: Frank Cass, 2000.

Herring, George C. *America's Longest War: the United States and Vietnam, 1950-1975.* 2nd ed. New York: Alfred A. Knopf, 1986.

Hoffman, Bruce. *Inside Terrorism.* New York: Columbia University Press, 1998.

Horne, Alistair. "The French Army and the Algerian War." *Regular Armies and Insurgency.* Edited by Ronald Haycock. London: Croom Helm, 1979.

Huntington, Samuel P. *The Clash of Civilizations and the Remaking of World Order.* New York: Simon & Schuster, 1996.

Kepel, Gilles. *Jihad: the Trail of Political Islam.* Translated by Anthony F. Roberts. Cambridge, MA: The Belknap Press of Harvard University Press, 2002.

Kitson, Frank. *Low-Intensity Operations.* London: Faber and Faber, 1971.

Lapping, Brian. *End of Empire.* New York: St. Martin's Press, 1985.

Leitenberg, Milton. *Assessing the Biological Weapons and Bioterrorism Threat*. Carlisle Barracks, PA: U.S. Army War College, Strategic Studies Institute, 2005.

Lenin, Vladimir . "Where to begin?" *Lenin Collected Works*, vol. 5. Moscow: Foreign Languages Publishing House, 1961. Available at the Marxists Internet Archive, http://www.marxists.org/archive/lenin/works/1901/may/04.htm.

Lewis, Bernard. *What Went Wrong?: the Clash between Islam and Modernity in the Middle East*. New York: Harper Perennial, 2003.

Mao Tse-Tung. "Report of an Investigation into the Peasant Movement in Hunan," March 1927, from *Selected Writings of Mao Tse-tung*, vol. 1. Beijing: Foreign Languages Press, 1963. Available at Marxists Internet Archive, http://www.marxists.org/reference/archive/mao/selected-works/volume-1/mswv1_2.htm.

Mockaitis, Thomas R., *British Counterinsurgency, 1919-1960*. London: Macmillan, 1990.

———. *British Counterinsurgency in the Post-Imperial Era*. Manchester, UK: Manchester University Press, 1995.

Nassar, Jamal R. *Globalization and Terrorism: the Migration of Dreams and Nightmares*. New York: Rowan and Littlefield, 2005.

Nechaev, Sergei. *The Revolutionary Catechism*. 1868. Online version. http://www.bellum.nu/literature/nechayev001.html.

Pimlott, John. "The French Army," in *Armed Forces and Modern Counterinsurgency*. Edited by Ian Beckett and John Pimlott. New York: 1985.

Rapoport, David. "The Four Waves of Modern Terrorism." *Attacking Terrorism: Elements of Grand Strategy*. Edited by Audrey Kurth Cronin and James M. Ludes. Washington, DC: Georgetown University Press, 2004.

Risen, James. *State of War: the Secret History of the CIA and the Bush Administration*. New York: Free Press, 2006.

Rudé, George. *Revolutionary Europe, 1783-1815*. New York: Harper & Row, 1964.

Shipler, David K. *Arab and Jew: Wounded Spirits in a Promised Land*. New York: Penguin, 1987.

Short, Anthony. *The Communist Insurrection in Malaya, 1948-1960*. New York : Muller, 1975.

Smith, Charles. *Palestine and the Arab-Israeli Conflict*. 5th ed. New York: Bedford/St. Martins, 2004.

Stern, Jessica. *Terror in the Name of God: Why Religious Militants Kill*. New York: Harper Collins, 2003.

Thornton, Thomas P. "Terror as a Weapon of Political Agitation," in *Internal War: Problems and Approaches*. Edited by Harry Eckstein. Westport, CT: Praeger, 1964.

Tonge, Jonathan. *Northern Ireland Conflict and Change*. New York: Pearson/Longman, 2002.

Weimann, Gabriel. *How Modern Terrorism uses the Internet*. Washington, DC: U.S. Institute of Peace, 2004.

Zuhur, Sherifa. *A Hundred Osamas: Islamist Threats and the Future of Counterinsurgency*. Carlisle Barracks, PA: Strategic Studies Institute, U.S. Army War College, 2005.

Articles

Ackerman, Gary, and Cheryl Loeb. "Much Ado Over Anthrax." *San Diego Tribune*, October 21, 2001, http://cns.miis.edu/pubs/other/muchado.htm.

Barrett, Chris L., Stephen G. Eubank, and James P. Smith. "If Smallpox Strikes Portland . . .," *Scientific American* (March 2005).

Bowyer Bell, J., "An Irish War," *Small Wars and Insurgencies* 1, no. 3 (December 1990): 244.

Clauset, Aaron, and Maxwell Young,. "Scale Invariance in Global Terrorism." physics/0502014. Cornell University Library e-prints in Physics, Mathematics, Computer Science and Quantitative Biology, http://arxiv.org/PS_cache/physics/pdf/0502/0502014.pdf (accessed March 6, 2006).

Dunham, Steve. "Mass Transit Defends Itself," *Journal of Homeland Security* (March 2002), http://www.homelandsecurity.org/newjournal/articles/dunhammasstransit.htm.

Giraldo, Jeanne K., and Harold A. Trinkunas. "The Political Economy of Terrorist Financing and State Responses: A Comparative Perspective." (unpublished manuscript of forthcoming book).

Handwerk, Brian. "Female Suicide Bombers: Dying to Kill." *National Geographic News online* (December 13, 2004). http://news.nationalgeographic.com/news/2004/12/1213_041213_tv_suicide_bombers.html.

Hassan, Nasra. "Are you ready? Tomorrow you will be in Paradise . . .." *Times Online*, July 14, 2005, http://www.timesonline.co.uk/article/0,,7-1692606,00.html.

Haykel, Bernard. "Radical Salafism: Osama's Ideology." http://muslim-canada.org/binladendawn.html#copyrightauthor.

Huntington, Samuel P. "Is there a Clash of Civilizations?" *Foreign Affairs* 7, no. 3 (Summer 1993): 22–28.

"Is Islamism a Threat? A Debate." *Middle East Quarterly* 6, no. 4 (December 1999), http://www.meforum.org/article/447.

Kelly, Henry. "Dirty Bombs, a Response to the Threat." *The Journal of the Federation of American Scientists* 55, no. 2 (March/April 2002), http://www.fas.org/faspir/2002/v55n2/dirtybomb.htm.

Most, Johann. "Attack is the Best Form of Defense," *Freiheit* (September 13, 1884). Available online at "Anarchy Archives: an Online Resource Center on the History and Theory of Anarchism." http://dwardmac.pitzer.edu/Anarchist_Archives/bright/most/attack.html.

Nasr, Hossein. "Spiritual Significance of Jihad." *Islamicity*, http://www.islamicity.com/articles/Articles.asp?ref=IC0407-2391.

"Online Support Grows for Iraq's 'Prince of Cutthroats." *Taipei Times*, October 6, 2004, http://www.taipeitimes.com/News/world/archives/2004/10/06/2003205773.

Palti, Leslie. "Combating Terrorism While Protecting Human Rights." *UN Chronicle* (online edition), vol. XLI (November 4, 2004), http://www.un.org/Pubs/chronicle/2004/issue4/0404cont.htm.

Panja, Tariq. "Analysts Say London Bombings Inexpensive." ABC News International, January 3, 2006.

Posner, Richard. "The 9/11 Report: a Dissent." *The New York Times Book Review,* August 29, 2004.

Propst, Rod. "Enhancing Disaster Management through an All-Hazards Continuity-of-Operations Continuum." *Journal of Homeland Security* (March 2006).

Regan, Tom. "Terrorism and the 'Net'." *Christian Science Monitor,* October 7, 2004, http://www.csmonitor.com/2004/1007/dailyUpdate.html?s=rsst.

Rotella, Sebastian. "Who Guided London's Attackers?" *Los Angeles Times,* March 6, 2006.

"Terrorist Activities on the Internet." *Terrorism Update* (Winter 1998). Anti-Defamation League website, http://www.adl.org/terror/focus/16_focus_a.asp.

"When Deadly Force Bumps into Hearts and Minds." *Economist* 374, no. 8047 (January 1, 2005): pp 30–32.

Williams, Phil. "Warning Indicators and Terrorist Financing." In Giraldo and Trinkunas, "Political Economy of Terrorist Financing."

Web Sites

Centers for Disease Control and Prevention. http://www.cdc.gov/.

———. *Bacillus Anthracis,* briefing, Oct. 31, 2001. http://www.bt.cdc.gov/agent/anthrax/SlideSetAnthrax.pdf.

———. "Bioterrorism Overview." http://www.bt.cdc.gov/bioterrorism/overview.asp.

———. *Frequently Asked Questions About Smallpox.* http://www.bt.cdc.gov/agent/smallpox/disease/faq.asp.

———. *Questions and Answers about Ebola Hemorrhagic Fever.* http://www.cdc.gov/ncidod/dvrd/spb/mnpages/dispages/ebola/qa.htm.

Central Intelligence Agency. http://www.cia.gov/.

———. *CIA World Fact Book, 2006.* http://www.cia.gov/cia/publications/factbook/index.html.

———. *Special Report of the Special Advisor to the DCI on Iraq's Weapons of Mass Destruction,* 2004. https://www.cia.gov/cia/reports/iraq_wmd_2004/glossary.html.

Director of National Intelligence. Mission Statement. http://www.dni.gov/aboutODNI/mission.htm.

———. "Brief NIC History." http://www.dni.gov/nic/NIC_history.html.

Federal Bureau of Investigation. http://www.fbi.gov/.

———. "Protecting America Against Terrorist Attack, A Closer Look at the FBI's Joint Terrorism Task Forces." http://www.fbi.gov/page2/dec04/jttf120114.htm.

———. Terrorist Screening Center, Mission Statement. http://www.fbi.gov/terrorinfo/counterrorism/mission.htm.

Federation of American Scientists (FAS). http://www.fas.org/.

Islam City. http://www.islamicity.com/articles/Articles.asp?ref=IC0407-2391.

Memorial Institute for the Prevention of Terrorism (MIPT) Terrorism Knowledge Base. http://www.tkb.org/Home.jsp.

National Counterterrorism Center, "About the National Training Center," http://www.nctc.gov/.

———. Task List, http://www.nctc.gov/about_us/how_we_do.html.

North Atlantic Treaty Organization. http://www.nato.int/.

Office of the Director of National Intelligence. http://www.dni.gov/.

U.S. Department of Homeland Security. http://www.dhs.gov/.

———. Fact Sheet, Securing US Ports http://www.dhs.gov/dhspublic/interapp/press_release/press_release_0865.xml.

———. "Undertakings of the Department of Homeland Security, Bureau of Customs and Border Protection," 11 May 2004. http://www.dhs.gov/interweb/assetlibrary/CBP-DHS_PNRUndertakings5-25-04.pdf.

U.S. Department of State. http://www.state.gov/.

White House. "Fact Sheet: Plots, Casings, and Infiltrations Referenced in President Bush's Remarks on the War on Terror." http://www.whitehouse.gov/news/releases/2005/10/20051006-7.html.

Index

About the Author

THOMAS R. MOCKAITIS is Professor of History at DePaul University in Chicago. As a consultant for the Center for Civil-Military Relations at the Naval Postgraduate School (Monterey, California), he also teaches government responses to terrorism at venues around the world. He is an expert in insurgency, counterinsurgency, peace operations, terrorism, unconventional war, and civil-military cooperation and a frequent media commentator on those subjects. His most recent book is *Grand Strategy in the War on Terrorism* (co-edited with Brian Rich, 2003).